On Being Human

Ernest Dyer

Published by New Generation Publishing in 2022

Copyright © Ernest Dyer 2022

First Edition

ISBN: 978-1-80369-094-0

www.newgeneration-publishing.com

New Generation Publishing

Contents

Chapter 1: Some existential conditions

'If I could enclose all the evil of our time in one image, I would chose this image that is familiar to me: an emaciate man, with head dropped and shoulders curved, on whose face and in whose eyes not a trace of a thought is to be seen.'

Primo Levi ('If This is a Man')

As individuals we, in a sense, 'find ourselves' within existence. During the process of growing into our lives a sense of our presence in the world invariably percolates into our consciousness. The intimate sense of this within-ness being realised when we reflect upon our presence as but a moment in space and in time within some curiously fluid, if matrix-like, set of experiential processes. A within existence that is irredeemably impacted when, for most at around the age of fifteen years, we become aware of our own mortality – that we too will die; invoking a profound realization of our own loss. We can of course at least try to pass lightly through the experience of life, focusing on fairly narrow life-aims drawn from connections to family, friends, hobbies, religion, travel, career, being 'entertained', and similar. And many of the world's people live in such difficult circumstances that engaging in more philosophical reflection is unrealistic; no doubt mostly only likely to stimulate despair rather than insight, nor even to gain some consolation. But for some of us a lot of the time, and I suspect for most of us at some time, more insistent questions about existence intrude; when, in imagination, we project beyond our more immediate experiences.

In what follows I attempt to articulate this reflective attitude in terms of three questions used to project our perspective beyond the immediacies of our lives: Why do I exist? – How do I exist? – What is my future? Complimentary to these more personal questions, the philosopher Immanuel Kant posed three more metaphysical rather than existential questions on behalf of humankind as a whole – What can we know? – What should we do? – What can we hope? This essay is intended to encompass both types of such insistent questions.

The renowned Greek philosopher Plato suggested that: '..... the origin of philosophy is Wonder.'

And wonder, whilst in certain experiential situations (say contemplating the starry sky or the birth of a child) can feel emotionally overwhelming, can also generate curiosity (the 'whys'), which can in turn lead to speculation and so serve as a source for at least some provisional answers, and to the generation of further more specific questions to be considered. Such has been the intellectual journey of humanity. Wonder is only but temporarily satisfied, and is born anew with each generation.

We might consider that Kant's own intellectually magnificent attempt to address the questions he posited (especially in his three 'Critiques') goes far beyond what we ourselves would be able to produce. But Kant's was an attempt that, with its emphasis on synthesis rather than a more dynamic consideration of the human condition, allows a sense that he neglected some more phenomenal aspects of experience. And as he was working in the eighteenth century he would have been unaware of some key scientific, potentially perspective changing, developments realised in the nineteenth century and later; not least the theory of evolution[1]. But his work had set a speculative standard to stimulate the work of others, providing intellectually broad shoulders upon which others stood to perhaps see further.

Consideration of these types of question, and more generally the ground of curiosity (the 'wonder') from which they arise, has a recorded history that conventionally takes us back to some Greek philosophers living about 2,500 years ago. These would certainly have been building on now mostly unrecorded work of Egyptian, Babylonian, and other Middle Eastern, proto-

---

[1] In his work Kant did quote the precociously perceptive Johann Gottfried Herder (1784) who early in the modern period highlighted the importance of upright walking in early humankind, noting : 'Let us pause for a moment to contemplate with gratitude this sacred work of art, this blessing which enabled our race to become human, and to wonder at it as we perceive the new organization of forces which arose out of man's erect stature and as we see that it was through this alone that man become man.' ('Kant Political Writings', 1970, ed. H.S.Reiss, p201)

philosophers. And Indian and Chinese thinkers were also engaged in what might broadly be termed philosophical speculation as early as the second millennium BCE – if this was more influenced by religious metaphysics than would be classical period Greeks. But surely such reflective considerations would have been an aspect of the human condition back to early humankind circa. 50,000 y.b.p. When the Homo species level of awareness had more clearly gained the modern human evolutionary mode of 'self-consciousness'.

Some time long ago, at a location or locations unknown, some species of Homo had evolved to the stage where they could reflect beyond the immediacies of their own lives. To consider their experiences in more abstract terms – to universalize the particular, to consider in terms of metaphors and analogies, to offer description in the absence of the described. A new threshold in the evolution of consciousness (as information-processing) had emerged from within evolutionary bio-dynamics. So allowing the cognitive conditions for the solitary thinker, one intensely focused on mind-bound distance images, peering sightless into the mystery of existence, seeking insight or at least some sense of cognitive resolution of the reconcilable and the acceptance of the continuing mysteries. A profoundly human image of the reflecting individual, just as those such as the suckling mother, fierce warrior, laughing child, entwined couple, concentrating craftsperson; and similar iconic motifs of humanness that echo down the generations. If this novel mode of thinking developed from about 50,000 y.b.p. it would take to about 600 BCE for Eastern and Western civilizations to begin to more obviously clarify and record such types of speculation.

When engaging in philosophical speculation we mostly aspire to apply a form of thinking broadly termed rational. A form that endeavours to approach its subject-matter in terms of: verifiable claims, logical consistency (if not the ratiocinated forms of symbolic logic), conceptual and relational coherence, a more general narrative consistency, and at best exhibiting the more elusive element of reason as 'wisdom'.

The political philosopher Hannah Arendt (Vol. I 'Thinking', 1978, p69) refers to Kant's conception of 'reason's need' – as:

'......the inner impulse of that faculty to acknowledge itself in

3

speculation.'

Rational is a rather archaic term but it does encompass elements that we can ourselves aspire to. Indeed, the element of 'insight' might be an aspect of both the rational forms and the religious modes involved in metaphysical speculation. But religious metaphysics unashamedly involves (and indeed is sustained by) the acceptance of the mythological, the miraculous, the unverifiable, and a more general lack of sensible coherence; both within and between religions. Each religion in its most conventional form, and all religions taken as a whole, offer explanatory frameworks that would fail to convince if the elements of rational analysis noted above were to be applied to their descriptions, explanations, and interpretations.

The very incredibility of religious explanations (of a god's involvement in the world, and of 'life' beyond death) might underlie their attraction for believers. We can identify elements of religion, if mostly in a more abstract sense, in much of philosophy, if increasingly less so from about 1750 CE; the period noted as the 'Enlightenment'. Even before this time religious influence had more-often been due to assumed social expectations. The gods were usually left as some more intellectually detached background condition, sustaining the all, but mostly separated from reasoning on more cogent aspects of the human situation. Historically, speculation in relation to the type of questions posed earlier became intellectually more credible when it finally eschewed the influence of religious modes of thinking.

Reasoning as a method-based activity can be applied to progressing evil ends as well as for good intentions; so in this abstract sense it is a neutral intellectual 'tool'. Having indicated this, I will come back to consider the implications, and adjustments necessary to foster positive outcomes, towards the end of the essay. For now I will just suggest that good and evil are not opposites. The conditions for good should simply be neutral, the 'norm. Evil is the disruption of the normal that we should aspire to. The absence of evil is but the mundane normality, the good is something pertaining that is more special than even the norm.

As Martin Buber suggested: 'Good and evil are not each others opposites like right and left. The evil approaches us like a whirlwind, the good as direction'.

4

It is conventional, and for my own purpose adequate, to note the early philosophers Thales, his student Anaximander, and his own student Anaximenes, as being the precursors of a body of speculative philosophy broadly labelled as 'Classical Greek'. A body whose primary enterprise in speculative reason was developed during a 500 odd year period beginning about 2,600 y.b.p. A period that saw reason applied initially to understanding the natural world, personal morality, and political organization, then widening to encompass the human condition more generally, with significant advances being made in areas such as ethics, logic and debating skills, metaphysics, and early science. All of these being exemplified in the combined work of Socrates, Plato, and Aristotle. Although of course, many others made their own original contributions at that time. The foundations of Western philosophy were laid within but 500 years, and for much of the subsequent time, extending down today, the shadow of some of these early philosophers continued to be cast over philosophical endeavours; if much less so during the last century.

Since the early Greeks some stand out Western philosophers would include: Rene Descartes, David Hume. Immanuel Kant, George Hegel, Edmund Husserl, John Dewey, Martin Heidegger, Bertrand Russell, Ludwig Wittgenstein, and John-Paul Sartre. This selection being admittedly personal, quite partial, and showing obvious male-orient bias; giving insufficient account of women philosophers, an absence due significantly to their historical intellectual suppression set within wider conditions of social oppression. Also missing are particular Chinese, India, Middle- Eastern, Persian, and African, philosophers who from as far back as 1500 BCE (Chinese and Indian) made significant contributions to the store of humankind's philosophical insights.[2]

My selection also ignores much of the philosophy in the

---

[2] Given the commonality of human psychology and a similarity of personal and civil experience it is hardly surprising that non-theistic philosophy in these regions has produced comparable work in epistemology, logic, ethics, and metaphysics, to their western contemporaries; if arguably with the implications being less developed. In addition, there is evidence to suggest early (first millennium BCE) interaction, certainly between India and the Middle-East, and probably also between China and these.

fourth quarter of the twentieth and the early decades of the twenty-first centuries, when advances were admittedly made in such areas as formal logic and the numerous approaches that can be, if some liberally, subsumed under the headings of analytic, hermeneutic, structuralist, post-structuralist and other modern and post-modern forms. Forms that mostly share a focus on meaning as presented and as interpreted, and the relevance of personal, social, and political, contexts for these. For myself, there is a general more critical value with these approaches that highlights their important combined contribution to metaphysical speculation rather than the work of any particular outstanding individuals.

Historically, the activity of philosophizing can generally be grouped into theoretical approaches, or rather similar sets of ideas that exhibit a sense of coherence. Although there have been some usefully provocative 'outliers' to the traditional grouping; with Henri Bergson, Friedrich Nietzsche, and Arthur Schopenhauer, being the more obvious. Some primary, if crude, groupings would be: idealism, empiricism, romanticism, pragmatism, logical positivism, analytic philosophy, phenomenology, existentialism, linguistic philosophy, structuralism, post-structuralism, modernism, and post-modernism. Each of which can offer wide-ranging descriptive and analytic types of explanatory frameworks and/or methods for considering aspects of the human condition.

Is this prolix range of quite different explanatory frameworks – most quite assertively set out - a critical weakness in philosophy; one redolent of un-admitted ignorance or perhaps more obvious intellectual egotism? Or rather than this, does it simply reflect the elusive complexity of the Reality within which we exist and the stage of intellectual development that we have currently reached – a stage reflecting some cognitive limitations characteristic of the self-conscious level of our species evolution.

The history of philosophy on a global scale has been an eons-long attempt to investigate the informational depths of the Reality we experience as being confronted with but which, ambiguously, we are ourselves within. An investigation engaged in by numerous philosophers, each setting out with different primary assumptions which then significantly influence any

6

descriptive/analytic process.

If considered positively we can accept that each philosophical grouping (school/approach) offers some level of insight into the condition as probed from a different perspective, with each being based on different assumptions of what aspects of the condition to highlight. Kant himself saw his own speculative system as an attempt to bring different philosophical insights together in a coherent way. More recent attempts – such as those of the Logical Positivists and the early Wittgenstein – were also made to overcome this multiplicity of approaches and place philosophy on a single methodological approach, not least by dismissing metaphysics altogether (as being nonsensical), and doing so primarily by focusing on language use and truth conditions.

The historian of philosophy Fredrick Copleston (Vol. VII, 1963, p422), when focusing on fundamental differences in some nineteenth century philosophical systems, considered a view that: 'The exaggerations in a philosophical system serve a useful purpose. For it is precisely the element of striking and arresting exaggeration which serves to draw attention in a forcible way to the basic truth that it is contained in the system.' He gives as examples: Marx on 'exaggerating' the importance of economic conditions and Nietzsche on 'exaggerating' the will to power as a fundamental dynamic in human life. Copleston suggests that for this view: '......it may be that each philosophy expresses a truth, an apprehension of a real aspect of reality or of human life and history and that these truths are mutually complementary.' That the accumulated exaggerations if taken together, would allow some revelatory insight into the human condition. Copleston considers this view in the context of Johann Fichte's claim of philosophy being the fundamental science. Unsurprisingly assumed by Fichte to be exemplified by his own system.

Can we allow that each 'exaggeration' can stand alone and, taken individually, each contributes to a valid body of knowledge; their intellectual credibility being sourced in some fine-grained original insight. I don't necessarily disagree with this somewhat optimistic view (if one that has more than a whiff of the apologetic about it), but I continue to view the range of

7

distinctly different philosophical systems as problematic in terms of the credibility of the discipline, if a seemingly inevitable aspect of individuals endeavouring to probe the metaphysical. I would suggest an alternative (possibly even more speculative) source of difference, and this would shift our perspective to the very horizon of Reality itself; to where lies the leading edge of humankind's evolutionary development.

Each philosopher (at their best as 'model practitioners') applied themselves to their own experience of the world and drawing on this they have endeavoured to systematically formulate and then set out ideas that take us beyond everyday experience in order to extend the boundary of our understanding, or to improve the intellectual tools for progressing this. A form of 'adaptation' to their experience that makes more sense if it brings order to the often dissonant information (ontologically mysterious in the sense of being veiled) that is the subject-matter of metaphysical speculation.

Just as biological adaptation produced organisms that advanced towards ever more powerful information processing systems, so philosophy (and in a different way the sciences) has traditionally encompassed the adaptive growth-bud of self-consciousness itself; so a behavioural adaptation responding to species need. In pushing up against this, the unknown (not necessarily unknowable), some form of philosophical system could emerge to take us further 'forward'; meanwhile, contending types of interpretive system have been involved in the struggle for intellectual primacy – perhaps a 'fittest' philosophical system will emerge in due course, so taking humankind to a higher (in information processing terms), indeed bio-transcendental, mode of understanding; or at least clarifying our presence in the world.

Copleston (ibid, p428 ish) notes that criticism of conflicting philosophical systems could be misplaced, for him an objection that is only valid if '......philosophy, to be justified at all, should be a science.' Contrary to this, for him: if '.....we understand the true function of metaphysics as being that of awakening man to an awareness of the enveloping Being in which he [sic] and other finite existents are grounded.' Then the objection is overcome. And that there being: '... different personal decipherings of Being is only what one ought to expect.'

The form of the information considered by philosophers is (primarily in relation to the extent of its abstraction from direct experience) not amenable to the terminological and factual consensus of the sciences; more especially the natural sciences. Where claims, descriptions, and explanations, can be expressed in mutually compatible forms; being compatible in the sense that scientists not only share a quite standardised training system they also share tacit and actual assumptions about how the world 'operates', and a common terminology drawn from these. Allowing them to more easily negotiate the relevance of new information and so more easily assimilate aspects of this within enduring wider interpretive frameworks.

Within philosophy, so many key concepts are liable to varying interpretations that in a sense philosophical, especially metaphysical, systems see debates being conducted in what are in a semantic sense different 'languages'. The meaning of words, propositions, and statements, are not fixed. They are liable to interpretation, and interpretation is liable to subjective fluidity; with meaning requiring clarity and generous negotiation if progress is to be made. And 'generous negotiation' over meanings has not been a characteristic of most philosophical disagreements.

For more mundane aspects of being human we can consider progress to have been made in the clarification of issues involved in: ethics, morality, epistemology, logic, and in reasoning procedures more generally. But for now we lack any secure explanatory (or even descriptive) insight into ultimate Reality and we can only note the history of philosophical speculation as producing tentative suggestions on the meaning (or conceptual content) of Being – even if we do seem to 'glimpse' possible clues for fruitfully investigating this, we currently also lack the vocabulary necessary to express it.

There is no correct or adequate system of philosophy that fully explains, or even describes, the human condition, each just at best gives insight from different perspectives, but all are there with the possibility of contributing to a debate that continues. Certainties are for religions; provisional explanations and descriptions (and analytics) are the products of authentic reflection. The hermeneutic (interpretative) potential of reason can be deployed to draw up human truths from that deep reservoir of wisdom that is there in the Reality we inhabit, the wisdom that has been articulated in more enlightened 'moments' throughout human history. Reasoning based on humanistic assumptions has the potential to provide the articulated receptacle from which we can draw profound human truths to the surface.

A common methodological approach in philosophy has been the wish to begin with some 'foundational' position - Of that which I can be certain (Descartes) – The dialectical starting point of 'being.....' (Hegel) – The phenomenon in itself (Husserl) – The problematic of personal existence in the world (Sartre) – The problematic of our 'lived being' within 'ontological Being' (Heidegger) – The problematic process of interpretation (hermeneutics more generally) – As well as the implications of language taken up by a number of individuals who were especially prominent in the second half of the twentieth century.

My own quite modest ideas on the human condition have a similar sense of a 'starting point', with my also asking the reader to bear with me when I begin my speculations from a novel starting point rather than more obviously developing ideas already set out by others.

If you are prepared to consider your life beyond the immediacies of the everyday and the reassuring explanations offered by religions for our lives, I ask that you consider yourself to have in a sense 'found yourself within existence'. That you are confronted with complexity overlying mystery as a unique centre of an awareness that will probably last for a relatively short time of – a mere 70 odd years lived on a tiny planet within a visible Universe 91 billion light years across and 13.8 billion years old. With our earth being one of eight planets orbiting an average sized star that is but one of very approximately 250 billion stars in our own galaxy and this but one of 100-200 billion (possibly many more) galaxies in the Universe. In this context, to even describe our lives as but a 'flicker' in space-time seems an over-generous exaggeration. But in the context of our own sense of being our, if brief, window on awareness (a life as but a 'sigh between two eternal silences' – as a traditional Irish saying goes) can be of vital relevance to our reflective selves.

This idea of selves as centres of awareness – whilst invariably entangled in networks of social relationships – presupposes individuality; a chronological nexus of accrued past experience, a more present sense of self, and an outlook that includes possible futures. This profound conundrum, of unique individualities entangled with a social nexus within a wider sense of space/time immensity, is the very stimulatory conditions for philosophical speculation. So stimulated, but with quite modest ambitions, I set off on my own speculative journey, one seeking to offer a description of some key elements of our experience within a framework that also seeks to provide a methodology for interpreting specific issues and hopefully, in doing so highlight ideas that might in turn stimulate the reader to progress beyond my own limited analysis.

I begin by positing the ontological mode of presence termed Being – a mode that provides a time-less, space-less conditionality; unformed yet a source of our individual be-ing, of our own individual presence in the world. Simply put, Being is ontological.....be-ing is existential. This is not dissimilar to Martin Heidegger's concepts of Being and Dasein, but hopefully without the sometimes difficult terminology, associated conceptual vagueness[3], and problematic relationships, that his are set in. My own concepts are intended to provide an instrumental framework within which we can set out a more specific consideration of the human condition.

To invoke a sense of Being..... think about the mode's condition in its universality – its past, its present, its future as encapsulated in the idea of a presence – but not in terms simply of facticity, more as a creative source of our experience. Our own be-ing expresses our personal entanglement as an existence within Being; the 'flicker' in space-time, already noted, during which our lives emerge. Lives as but tiny perturbations in the awesome flowing eternity of Being. But perturbations in the

---

[3] Some might consider this to be a positive aspect of Heidegger's concepts and that the rest of his outline (in his book 'Being and Time') provides some substance to these initial modes.

fabric of Being that assume enormous relevance in each of our own lives as we reflect on our hopes, fears, expectations, and our experience more generally.

Being, is the ontological backcloth against which our reflective lives are conditioned; if 'be-ing' is itself conditioned by our experiential lives. The concept of Being – all encompassing characterised by semantic emptiness – it has to be admitted trembles uneasily on the edge of the meaningless. It is a concept that directs us to a mode of possibility for all experience. I pose Being, and indeed my whole exposition, in terms of heuristic value – not as some ultimate truth. Heidegger has it that our humanness in characterised by our awareness of Being. He poses Being as a problem for us humans (as Dasein). But Being can provide a sense of a form, of placing a be-ing within a wider metaphysical context, or it could more mundanely represent the unknown beyond human understanding, and yet it offers a sense of presence that envelops us in our own finitude.

In the previous section I employ the stylistic device of inserting a hyphen within a word e.g. be-ing. This might seem a rather contrived usage, aping the style of philosophers such as Heidegger and Sartre, both prolix users; I will employ it as judiciously as I can. I do so in order to highlight that the word affected has a very different intended meaning than the same word printed as normal usage. The hyphen is inserted to indicate the importance of both of the syllables being separated e.g. be-ing is to emphasize that a person 'be' is 'ing' the world in an interactive, cognitive, sense, not just as a general sense of being present, here or there. Three other stylistic devices employed are: the use of a capital letter to begin a word other than at the start of a sentence or other normal usage e.g. Being. The highlighting of a word by enclosing it within ' 's e.g. 'real' - and the use of bold type for one or a series of words e.g. **provisionalism.** Each of these devices is intended to draw a reader's attention to a word as having a sense other than conventional usage. I use four rather than simply one device because the sense of meaning I wish to invoke differs with each type of usage. I hope the difference becomes clear, or at least acceptable, as the reader experiences the context of each usage. The use of these devices probably reflects my own linguistic limitations, if my conscious intention is to give a more lucid originality to my descriptive analysis.

I also want to acknowledge that when undertaking any analysis touching on the metaphysical the language we use cannot cope with the sheer complexity it is struggling to describe, we are forced to use the same words to explain generally subtlety, but sometimes obviously, different situations.

As George Steiner noted on seeking words whose meaning has not been devalued by overuse: 'The spirit shuffles like a ragpicker in quest of words that have not been chewed to the marrow, that have kept something of their secret life despite the mendacity of the age.' (Steiner, 'Extraterritorial', 1976 ed., p29).

One can think of words such as 'hero', 'truth', 'democracy', 'socialism', and 'freedom', as prime examples of conceptual husks left with but faint echoes of originally intended meanings, taken from our own mendacious age. For the purpose of this essay we might also include 'mind' and 'real'.

The human condition is a mobile entity, psychologically involving an interlinked multiplicity of unconscious, preconscious, and conscious processes. Cultural evolution has led to changing perspectives, and therefore changing representations, on the meaning of be-ing within Being. We can accept that it is valid to outline a thorough-going philosophy of existence, rather than this search amounting to searching, in an immeasurably complex way (the history of metaphysical philosophy), for something that simply does not exist. That the question of 'truth' about existence, the how and why we came into exist, are, as some heirs to the logical positivist tradition and others might argue, meaningless.

Owing primarily to the evolving dimension of the human condition, any outline can as yet only be provisional. We can but aspire to progress the best possible analysis given the invariably limited nature of our knowledge and our ability to, in functional terms, order it most effectively in relation to our purpose.

The idea of purpose appears to impose a further limitation, a narrowing of focus, when it might be more useful to at least start with a more general approach to understanding the human condition. The latter being an approach which most past, and some present, philosophers at least appear to assume they take.

They mostly proceed as if one could reason from seemingly pre-suppositionless beginnings (Husserl determinedly so), letting some logically pure concepts arising from an initial encounter lead the student/practitioner/ commentator into the subject, then allowing more detailed reasoning to proceed from these. Descartes 'I think, therefore I am' is an early example during the modern period. Hegel's originating concept of being which then 'logically' gives rise to non-being, with the dialectical interplay between these two giving rise to becoming; a concept which both subsumes (sublates) being and not-being and, by overcoming their opposition, is something more. This is the triadic beginnings from which Hegel's vast, wide-ranging, speculative system is constructed.

I would unashamedly state my own purpose as being the wish to understand the human condition from a perspective of why there is 'evil' in the world, not as some assumed value-free analysis. What is it that inheres in 'human nature' that has caused, and continues to cause, so much misery and suffering in the world? From this my initial reflection upon the human condition, our encounter with-in Being, gives rise to four assumptions, revealing my intentional perspective which will become clearer as the essay progresses.

1) That each individual person has a unique experience of existence, that the subjective (experiential) is a fundamental fact of existence, there is no purely 'objective' area of experience, objectivity is a social construct, it's veracity being a matter of degree, of facts and relationships more or less subjectively interpreted.

2) Whilst accepting the above, that there is nevertheless an area of 'shared' experience which allows for communication, empathy, and other types of mutual understanding without which social, and any intellectual interaction, would be impossible. Also, within this sharable world has been distinguished (if only by degree) a type of knowledge that is at best as free as is possible from subjective involvement, as in some refined 'scientific' knowledge. But at its worst it is knowledge misused; masquerading under the cloak of some notional types

of objective knowledge linked to some supposed irrefutable truths. This can be knowledge used, sometimes for well-intentioned reasons, in areas of the social sciences, and less well-intentioned to support aspects of the most spurious of ideological theories. This last being summed up in the idea of an assumed 'objectively of the normative' often redolent within tribe, religion, community, class, ethnic, nation, and other such groupings.

3) That the concept of 'information' is critical to enable clarification of the implications of be-ing. Information being that 'semantic substance' of which we are actually or potentially aware, in the sense that any organism can act upon its environment in response to sensory, or as is the case with 'higher' organisms including the apes and human-beings, conscious, information. Information is what in general constitutes the substance of awareness and in more developed forms is processed by the human cognition.

I would contend that information is the sustaining dynamic expressed in the evolution of life; the material that all organisms have been biologically designed to process. Information being as fundamental as space-time and energy.

4) Following on from 3)...In my sense of the concept of 'information', human-beings have (as a bio-social species) evolved over long periods of time from the simplest form of 'information-processing' organisms - mere self-replicating packages of genetic material contained within cellular forms being the simplest - by identifiable stages of development represented in different biological species, into organisms able to process evermore complex information. In terms of human timescales, social then cultural evolution has clearly overlaid the biological. A necessary corollary being that there is no reason to think that bio-social evolution has ceased to be an influence on human life, and a great deal of circumstantial evidence to the contrary.

One significant implication of the prioritization of information is that the whole of Reality, all that we can know (possible and actual) - all facts, ideas, emotions, states of affairs, indeed all conceived and conceivable phenomena are constituted by their informational content - 'all' is information. I am suggesting that it would be useful to posit this as a key epistemic condition for human beings; as ontological fact and epistemological condition. Reductionist, yes but.......to include a reduction in an analysis would only be problematic if this is the whole procedure rather than only a beginning. Information sustains our constitution, life for each of us is experienced within circumscribed 'information fields' similar to gravitational fields in the sense of immersion, if without the more deterministic sense of the pull of a direction.

Considered in terms of function, organisms process information in order to maintain themselves within an environment. Information processing is an essential marker of evolutionary development, it being the overt dynamic. Human-beings (at the apex of the hierarchy in relation to information processing capacity) can perceive this 'substance' via the senses and can generate and manipulate more information via their more physiologically-related and their more thinking-related activities. Information can be viewed as being a spectrum of complexification, ranging from the just noticeable 'difference' in some (external or internal) sensory feature such as temperature, light, appetite, emotion, and similar, to the complex nexus of 'differences' that we would encounter with scientific knowledge and more generally the configurations of meaning-infused information that constitute most of the patterns of our conscious thinking.

J.Z.Young (1971) offered an estimate of the amount of information that can be involved in life. He noted the massive flow of information through a body – estimating that even a single bacterial cell has 10^{12} 'bits' of information flowing through it during its lifetime. The estimated sum of all sensory information flowing through the human central nervous system (CNS) over a lifetime of 10^{16}, with the brain's estimated storage capacity being 10^{10}-10^{11} 'bits' - quite staggering amounts.

For Claude Shannon (cited in P.Watson, 2016, 'Convergence', p399) on the link between information and thermodynamics: 'There is something about information that transcends the

16

medium that it is stored in. It is a physical property of objects akin to work or energy or mass..... Nature seems to speak in the language of information.' If Shannon's view of information was more computational ('bits') than my own more existential ('signs'- see below).

Information is the form of substance that facilitates communication (the exchange of 'difference') as minimal as interaction at the molecular level or as maximal as interaction at the level of human emotional and cognitive processes.

We are information-processing entities located within information-rich environments. Information can be viewed in quantitative and qualitative terms; as sense-data the quantitative is more relevant (but not circumscribed by this) and as meaning the qualitative is more relevant (but not defined by this), for humans and some other species these two are blended together within awareness. We can only know of our be-ing-within-Being due to our ability to process information at a certain level of awareness, one that involves an ability to hold information seemingly 'before' the mind....as memories, immediate considerations, imaginations, and as plans for the future. Representation and reflection characterize human consciousness.

Even given how far consciousness has developed, human-beings cannot provide satisfactory answers to the three insistent questions noted as the 'we' of our species, posed earlier - Why we exist? - How we exist? - What will become of our species? Insistent questions for those who contemplate the shimmering horizon of human existence lying beyond the strand-line of our everyday lives.

Providing that our species, or perhaps another emergent self-conscious species, survives (on earth or elsewhere in the Universe) what will those 'super-conscious' beings of 1,000, 10,000, 100,000 years in the future 'think', in relation to the three basic questions on existence outlined above.

Just consider that conscious brains (a biological enabling condition for conceptual thought) have increased in crude physical size alone from about 350 grams in weight to 1500 grams in but four or five million years of evolution. A period during which we evolved out of the cognitive limitations of our primate ancestors to gain the self-conscious mode of modern humankind. This increased capacity has provided a necessary condition for a qualitative 'advance' in our intellectual ability as compared with a 360 gram. brained chimpanzee or orang-utan.[4] And, party owing to the 'exponential' increase in knowledge over the last 50,000 or so years, the rate of intellectual advance of humankind, taken as a whole, is accelerating (if discontinuously). How will Reality and Being be understood and known by those, to us, potentially super-intelligences who could exist circa 1,000, 10,000 or even 100,000 years on? There are probably physiological limitations as to how far human brain-growth could reach. Although there is evidence that a significant amount of current human brain capacity is for the most part unused; memory capacity seems to have no limits re. encoding – if recall and processing speed can have significant limitations. But the potential of the continuing and rapid advances in artificial intelligence and cognitive modelling by computer programs -connectionism, pdp's, neural networks, quantum computing, etc. - certainly stimulate the imagination. For those that claim that the thinking power of 'biological wiring' in the brain cannot be replicated by silicon or other forms of 'wiring' in a box, I would suggest a cautionary approach. There will be a continuing increase in the processing power of all computer programs utilising nano-technology and quantum computing.

I cannot see any significant advances here in the replication of what G.A.Miller (1981) termed the 'human point of view', involving, feeling, willing, and knowing. And thinkers such as Roger Penrose, John Searle, and Maurice Edelman, in an accessible way for the general reader, have shown the theoretical problems of assuming we can replicate human consciousness with computer processing.

However computer science (as A.I.) need not be bound by any limitations in 'wiring', there is research now being carried out which involves growing neural networks. Let the informed

---

[4] Brain size is a crude measure of intellectual capacity, afterall, elephants and some other animals have much larger brains than humans. There is also the structural and neural complexity to consider – but brain size has been useful marker in relation to the evolution of primates and their assumed cognitive development.

imagination pursue this line of thought and one can conceive of a human-being connected to an information-processing extension that will not only improve the processing power but will give the qualitative rise in consciousness that moves the species to a radically new level of information processing ability - and so to a level of awareness that transcends the current human self-conscious mode. What was previously the realm of science fiction is absorbed into the advancing realm of scientific possibility.

In its simplest form information is just 'stimulating material', realised when a flexible threshold of sensory activation is passed. Such thresholds can be conscious and/or unconscious depending primarily on differential levels of awareness experiencing what is felt as incoming patterns of 'raw' sensory data.

The primary aim of philosophical endeavour is to clarify the conceptual material circumscribing aspects of experience: its content, relationships, and implications, and to re-present it fully formed defined and polished to the interested public. Whereas in everyday life we can get by with fairly general forms of conceptual material mostly untroubled by any more significant moral, political, and certainly metaphysical, implications.

The varying degree of abstraction of conceptual material is unrelated to any inherent features of the concepts themselves but rather to a range of factors related to the thinking person in the experiencing situation. To illustrate the flexible nature of conceptual material: we use the concept of freedom in ways, at one extreme being lose, the idea of walking around or of not being physically imprisoned, or the freedom to choose to walk, drive, or cycle to a workplace.

However, if we consider the concept more finely we need to take into account freedom in relation to economic exploitation or social oppression, or freedom of thought in a media-controlled world, which it might be argued imprisons us behind elusive but effective bars of ignorance – What the author Saul Bellow noted as the deep 'unknown' currents of newsworthy information ignored by the media in favour of surface ripples – more in-depth analysis often involves contentious questions of interpretation, implication, and bias.

When we enter upon a more abstract type of information processing, as in speculative philosophy in a formal sense, it is useful (of heuristic value) to introduce the idea of representation. This most obvious feature of information processing can of course be an element of many other mental activities, including religious reflection, and all of the more theoretical approaches in the social and natural sciences. Representations are abstract concepts taking a more fixed form (narrow or wide-ranging), they are that form of cognitive material which can be held before consciousness, to be considered and re-considered usually in relation to other representations - within conventional and coherent systems of wider representation. Re-presentations constitute the patternings of information that are held before the mind in images, language, or both, or even more contentiously as some forms of mentalease

The social psychologist Gillian Cohen ('Themes and Issues', Open University, 1994) suggests that representations are the 'stuff' of cognition, for Cohen: '.....they are what the system is designed to handle'.

The first three representations I would invoke together constitute 'self-consciousness'. Self-consciousness being that aspect of the mental that overlies, in a poorly understood interactive relationship, the more organic elements of being human. These representations (so each circumscribing relatively fixed forms of information) are: **Reality - Language - Thought**. They are in general, or rather in terms of the constituting information which each of these concepts seeks to represent, intermixed and interactively involved in consciousness. For the sake of analytic clarity I think it would be useful to view these three representations more as 'analytic tools' to be applied to circumscribing the humming world of experiential information constituting our psychological milieu. They are no more or less real than representations such as freedom, democracy, evil, etc. Similar to these, my representations also re-present something that is vitally important in our lives and, of more relevance to my own purpose they can be useful heuristic terms designed to progress an understanding of the human condition in terms of its psychological constitution.

I would begin by giving each of these conceptual

representations a provisional characteristic:

1. **Reality** - In terms of both the amount and types of information contained within it - as 'complex', potentially infinitely so.

2. **Language** - Although in use flexible and potentially creative - as 'synthetic'.

3. **Thought** - At all the permeable and interacting levels leading from the unconscious via the pre-conscious to the fully aware and vice versa - I define as 'intentional'.

These characteristics of – complex, synthetic, intentional - are intended only to be preliminary defining terms, i.e. reflecting the feature each representation possesses that is more determinate, and this therefore does not excluded the presence of other less determinant elements. I wish to highlight these three concepts because of their affective involvement with each other as they are subsumed in the more inclusive subjective concept of personal existence (be-ing). One can see this involvement more especially in fully conscious experience. Where information making up a part of Reality is structured according to available Linguistic frameworks, in conformity with the Intentional requirements of any subject. To take a simple example:

A person is consciously observing the sky at dawn. She is aware of trying to determine the likelihood of rain during the day ahead. This is her linguistically framed thought. Information is streaming in via her senses to consciousness from what is experienced as the external environment; in forms which are often influenced by pre- and un- conscious aspects of mind. The person structures and selects (mostly 'auto-consciously') from this mass of potentially available information according to the intentional substratum underlying and infusing the thought that has placed her in the 'sky observing' situation. In this case the possibility of spending the day in the vegetable garden. But the thought that has placed her in the sky observing situation can have a far more complex underlying nexus of intentionality. Including the wish not to go shopping with her partner, or to

21

have an excuse to not be in hearing distance of the telephone and so be unable to take an unwanted call from a friend/relative/workplace, or her belief that time spent gardening can offer some therapeutic respite from an otherwise turbulent emotional life, etc. etc. Rich layers of intentionality potentially implicated within the seemingly more superficial simplicity of any situation.

Few (especially British) philosophers seem to want to consider the messy area of individual psychological considerations, at least those involving intentionality, and tend to posit some 'ideal types' to populate their metaphysical systems when some actual human perspective, even in abstracted form, is necessary. It is easy to sympathize with the more conventional approach given that there are potentially over 7 billion different interpretive frameworks. With each one of these in a state of intentional fluxion as a person's experience proceeds and their life circumstances change; each one infused with uniquely formed intentional elements. And no doubt the deployment of ideal types to illustrate ideas has advanced understanding of some aspects of being human. But the human condition in its wholeness has to encompass individual psychology in all of its messy complexity (and indeed mystery). We must not lose sight of this limitation.

Reality, Language, and Thought, are but three aspects of a wholeness infusing and perhaps rather ambiguously creating each other at higher levels of self-consciousness. It is impossible to outline all the implications of their inter-involvement in awareness because we know so relatively little about it. But, as a pre-condition to an analysis, they can be usefully prized apart and considered in themselves, from a perspective which views them more as disembodied abstractions. This in order to gain at least some understanding of how elements of each constitute, in different ways, the mental awareness which is our existential 'window on the world'; constituting our sense of be-ing within it.

The very act of separation implies a purpose on my part, there can be no entirely objective analysis, there is always an affective intentional substratum. The motives underlying any purposive act of separation can be a determining factor in how analysis will proceed. The intentions I am conscious of derive from a wish to gain some understanding of the processes that constitute 'awareness' (the form taken by the conceptual material which is actively before the mind – and the preconscious material that is involved with this), and from this gives rise to, and can determine, the judgments we make and the subsequent actions we take. But as already noted, for the sake of methodological integrity I must emphasize that my conscious motives are inextricably connected to my conception of the human condition as problematic – one centred on the existence of 'evil'. Why is it present in human life? Why does its presence threaten the future of our species? What conditions need to pertain in order to eradicate the 'tendency towards evil', at least as much as would be possible at this stage of human evolution? Such questions provide the dynamic that generates the formulation of the intentions outlined above. It is felt by me as a deeper level of intention, providing the motive force to the more obviously stated intentions. So no assumed disinterested metaphysical speculations on the human condition.

I doubt that I would have taken to the study of philosophy as a teenager for any other reason than the felt need to answer the 'question of evil'. Any analysis that seeks to avoid discussion of the motives and intentions of the author can only ever be of limited value. So I tend towards the psychological (limitations and motivations) in my consideration of metaphysics rather than language as such or ontology as such.

The concepts themselves (R-L-T) are not of course 'objective entities' waiting to be revealed; one can imagine an analysis of the human condition using representations which are less obviously 'crude' than the three I posit. Each concept has its own genealogy, some dense accretion of meaning-rich interpretations that have left the informational context of each as being quite negotiable. Such is the nature of language that once concepts are formed they tend to appear like self-subsistent objects. But for me, the formulation of concepts of this type are elements deployed in but speculative attempts to gain an initial access to the human condition. I have a strong sense that when I am defining these abstract concepts and outlining their interaction I am forging 'tools' with which to further my understanding of the implications of being human.

So, prized apart and held up to the analytical light of reason I have Reality, Language and Thought. I will now suggest the sort of conceptual structures that can be revealed for each of them.

Firstly, we have Reality which I characterized earlier as 'complex'. A complexity arising from the 'all' which the content of Reality re-presents. Reality posited as a theoretical entity is 'all that there is and every relationship between things'. The only limit to Reality is set by the available informational content – and indeed this is ever-expanding. It becomes existentially limited because each person can only have awareness (and experience) of a relatively tiny fragment of it - their own 're-ality'. The content of Reality is information, from the barely significant to the most profound of 'differences'. For humans this being the semantic material which pervades our consciousness, ranging from just perceptible stimuli to highly abstract ideas, or simple-to-complex explanations about phenomena. I set no limits on the conceptual material potentially available for human beings to conceive of, whether real or unreal, actual or possible. Reality has drawn all the information ever produced into its presence.....so as the creation of information proceeds so Reality expands. Reality is the irreducible informational habitat for humankind.

Reality is an ever-present potential source of information, if seemingly just too big in scope to adequately conceptualize, just consider: the moment in time that a Roman soldier serving on the fringe of the Empire paid for his daily loaf of bread is a part of Reality, as is the unrecorded death of a insectivorous creature 200 million years ago, as is two sub-atomic particles colliding during the initial stage of the creation of the Universe, as is the amoeba ingesting microscopic food particles, as is the picking of a flower by a Chinese peasant to pass to his loved one on a spring morning in 1025 C.E., as is the mother admonishing her child for swimming if the Euphrates River circa 2,500 BCE, as is any leaf falling silently to the forest floor, as is the Supernova occurring 3 billion years ago...... and so on and so on. These being but a few of the more obviously circumscribed 'informed events'. And for each circumscribed moment we can posit an original event and a potentially endless multiplicity of representations of this.

Any such information-generating 'event' could be included; ones created out of difference and involving an exchange of energy at some level. The trillions and trillions of events (as micro-macro 'changes of state') occurring each second since the initial 'Big Bang'. With the 13.8 billion year-long infusion of information being expressed in the ways in which the Universe has developed as the rate of information-accumulation has accelerated and the informational complexity of circumscribed events has increased.

With human evolution and the ability to generate and record information the complexity reached a potentially new level - most obviously expressed in formulas describing states of relativity theory, quantum mechanics, and entropy, and in concepts such as 'Religion', 'Nation', 'Freedom', 'War', or 'Evil'. Taking informational complexity to a distinctly new level.

In addition to what might be considered as more conventionally accepted as 'real' information, there are also the more nebulous types of information. Not just the dragons, demons, fairies, cyclops, unicorns, ware-jaguars, ghosts, mermaids, and similar, but also the kaleidoscopic content of humankind's religious beliefs, encompassing the information on the miraculous, the mythical, the spiritual, the whole wealth of imagination-infused imagery. What can collectively endure in forms that we can find more useful is information related to cultural adaptations, civil construction, natural and social scientific knowledge, philosophy, political ideologies, medicine, agriculture, economics, and a range of other categories of information that we might term 'knowledge' that has accrued during humankind's historical experience. All together potentially contributing to enhancing 'consciousness', as it contributes to the formation of Reality. An information infused realm, most seemingly now permanently lost to us and yet much more continuing as available to be considered, whether historical event, scientific field of discovery, or using what we know to describe a possible past set of circumstances or to plan a possible future. By posing such an expansive idea of Reality I am seeking to invoke a sense of wonder in the reader but also to reinforce the fact that information is the medium of consciousness as it is for the constitution of the Universe - along with mass, energy,

25

and space-time.

But does positing such an infinitely inclusive definition of Reality dissipate any heuristic value in it as an idea? In the sense that I posit a seemingly unmanageable amount, and in fact now mostly unknowable (lost in the vastness of the space-time) 'celestial oceans' of information, with evermore unmanageable amounts of information being added each day, indeed each second!

In terms of humankind's civil life it has been estimated (as noted by Hans Christian von Baeyer, 2003) that the volume of information being created doubles every three years; this significantly due to the ubiquitous information-generating WWW – although there might in the future be technological (processing and storage) constraints that would at least limit the pace of growth.

The value in positing the idea of a Reality encompassing a boundary condition for all of the information ever realized is that this allows us to envisage a vast pool of information where each 'circumscribed informative entity' ('sign-situation' - see below) can potentially, if not always practically, be returned to for further consideration – most obviously this might be some historical event, or when considering the formation of a planetary system, or the constitution of the habitat of a amphibious creature living some 100 million years ago. The infinite complexity (and indeed interrelatedness) of informational Reality is the fundamental back-cloth for understanding the inevitably provisional nature of the truth (in terms of implications) of the judgements we make and of the explanations we offer. One implication of noting information-based Reality as infinitely complex is the implied assumption that Reality itself is a circumscribed unity linking 'everything' together. This is the nub of the idealist philosophical position, with anything but the whole only being but relatively real. But even ignoring the question of the validity of the logic used to arrive at this idealist conclusion, it is one that freezes Reality into some featureless pure abstraction. Whereas the concept of provisionalism, set in the context of an infinitely complex information-rich Reality, allows the dynamism inherent in the essential nature of Reality to be acknowledged, indeed to be operationalized for more metaphysical considerations. The Reality I posit is information-rich in terms of all that there is; including the accrued, now vast, reservoir of humankind's evolutionary become cultural journey through time. Taking the forms of information that are theoretically or actually possible for humans to access.

Each species has a sensory information 'bandwidth' which circumscribes the form of information in terms of informational characteristics; basically of the sensory and the meaningful. Constituted for humans by the perceptual as in touch, hearing, smell, and sight, and conceptual as in self-conscious awareness and more reflective thinking. We know that, subject to individual variation, each human can only process information in certain forms and at a certain rate; if advancing technology, not least computing power, has significantly extended the range of informational complexity that can be processed. Even given the significant widening of the technologically enhanced information processing bandwidth that 21st century humans can deploy, we still can only in one life access a relative thin sliver of the all that there is available in Reality.

In its most basic form, information is conveyed via an electro-magnetic substrate (its material form) – it is realised in a change of 'state' in an entity or system – this being the source of the difference that can be noticed by sensory organisms (as perceived and conceived) - actually or potentially. In information technology we have information as 0s and 1s streamed in configurations that we can interpret as meaningful. In the human brain and wider nervous system single neurons operate in terms of on–off transmissions, but do so within interlinked more local networks of millions/billions of other neurons (and associated glial cells) signalling via on-off takes on a biologically unique mode of information processing. As a seemingly 'emergent property' of neural patternings – but this in a sense that merges the material with the immaterial, eluding our understanding of this in ways we do not yet have the language to express.

How does Reality differ from Being and personal re-ality from personal be-ing? The first two share a similar type of abstract presence and the second two share a similar type of existential presence (lived immediacy). I suggest Being as the universal predicate for life whereas Reality is the information available for be-ing (as consciousness). For us, neither has meaning without the other - the human is realised within the intersection of Being and Reality - but they do circumscribe different modes of human conditionality.

It might help to note that, simply expressed:

- Being is fundamentally ontological
- Reality is fundamentally informational
- re-ality is the cross section (fragment) of Reality that we, as individuals, access during our lives.
- be-ing is the personal mode of experiencing this re-ality.

After Being, Reality is from a general perspective the most abstract of all concepts, symbolizing every-thing we can possibly know; it has a similar abstract status to Being but is intended as being less personal. More akin to a medium of information wherein 'things' exist, so providing the source of semantic content for consciousness. A numinous ever-expanding boundary containing all 'entities' - all differences or changes of state - within it. From a more realised perspective Reality is the most concrete of concepts given that it is the inherent (necessary and sufficient) epistemological condition for all things. To be is to be <u>Real</u>; for humans to be conditioned by 'meaning'.

A commonly held view of our more everyday (personal) re-ality is that it is distinguishable from that which is un-real, that there are two 'realms' of personal experience. One containing solid entities and relationships between these, and the more explicit feelings and emotions of experience; usually experienced as having some external reference. The other being a sort of ephemeral world that can exist only in our heads, to be easily dismissed. Reality is contrasted with unreality, resulting in a bi-polarity of experience categorizing particular experiences according to judgments being made in terms of personal and/or social determinants. I consider this to be false dichotomy - between a real and an unreal world of experience – one that has led to a great deal of argument and misunderstanding and would maintain it to be of little value for productive speculative reason.

I would go further and suggest it to have little value even in

28

everyday usage. To give a simple example: A person who believes in a god which they consider to be real, whereas another, of more atheistic inclination, might judge the first person's belief to be real but the object of their belief i.e. a god, to be unreal, a mere fiction. The second person denies the status of reality to something of fundamental relevance in the life of the believer, hence the potential for misunderstanding or even antagonism. In any particular inter-personal experience we must endeavour to, as accurately as possible, ascertain that the parties to any agreement understand any area of 'Reality' at least to the extent that any disagreement between them (of: propositions, references, facts, relationships) is accepted on the same basis. The veracity of any belief for the atheist might include conditions requiring substantive evidence and narrative coherence, whereas perhaps for the religious believer what is required is unconditional faith in an historically constructed idea. If progress in communication between these two is to be achieved then attempts must be made to ensure that both parties feel they are talking about the 'same thing', at least sufficiently to be able to usefully engage. In the example this 'thing' being the god of a believer. It would be more fruitful if the believer and the atheist discussed the implication of holding or rejecting the existence of a god as this might relate to a shared preoccupation – such as cooperating to mitigate the expression of evil in the world.

Even on a simple functional level it can be more useful to judge events by the effects and other implications of any experience (a useful insight of 'pragmatism', if used with a degree of circumspection) rather than in accordance with how an observer might interpret them in relation to their own evaluation of real/unreal. For example, aspects of a dream, which is usually interpreted as being unreal could have a greater effect on someone (famously so with Moses' interpretation of Pharaoh's dreams in the Judaic story) than some more trivial but 'real' everyday experience. I do not wish to invoke any simplistic version of behaviourism here, to only judge human cognitive activity by observation of overt behaviour. Rather, I suggest that we not only observe the more obvious affects but also seek to understand the implications of the subject's experience-for-themselves.

Our insecurity in the face of the complexity and the uneasy variety of experience leads us to seek firmer ground of a 'real' Reality from which we can judge any experiences that are sufficiently different from this as 'unreal'. Even our own dreams (hopes and fears), often a central experience of our interior lives, we describe as unreal, and yet current understanding of the psyche show the interconnectedness of our dreams to our overall psychic life (un - pre - and self - consciousness), and the way we live in the world.

I suggest that we need to enlarge the concept of Reality to encompass all experience of which we can potentially be conscious; so not only that tiny cross-section of Reality (so re-ality) that we are directly conscious of. This more expansive concept of Reality is the 'all' of experience, no-thing is excluded, each-thing is but a particular manifestation of it, however insignificant or unreal it may initially seem to be. That we do not ever deny the other's 're-ality', instead that we only seek to identify the epistemological status of the other's conceptions and beliefs and the implications of holding these.

This conceptualization of Reality (as fragmented personal re-alities) attempts to express the potential value of all types of experience, including all the possible or actual content of the perceivable/conceivable. That which is usually considered 'real' and that 'unreal', everything and every possible relationship between things. An idea that seeks to represent the vast source (fluxion) of experience that the 'I' stands opposed to and at the same time, from a more essential perspective, is a part of. I am within the world as it is within me. In making Reality such an all-inclusive concept I might appear to have made it meaningless, vague, and to have rendered the concept useless for understanding. But, as I outline the concept, it is projected as an idea, suggested as a heuristic attempt to circumscribe the 'all' of 13.8 billion years of information creation and development, in particular within humankind's evolutionary become civil experience. All of the experienced and potentially experienceable information which forms humanly accessible Reality has an ever-expanding boundary determined by the stage of bio/psycho/social human evolution. The limited terrain of the humanly accessible Reality being that complex mass of information that is accessible (potentially) to the informational band-width of cognate human beings. If in practice this potential can never be fully realised. Apart from the fact that a single person cannot experience all that others experience (the ground for differential interpretation) we also have so many areas of human experience, high-energy physics being an obvious example, for which there is an extensive and necessary 'learning curve'.

An area of Reality which has undergone a veritable explosion in both amount and complexity is the area of more formal 'knowledge' - knowledge of the history of the Universe, the Earth, the whole of recorded human experience - knowledge of both the physical and social sciences - and similar areas of Reality which have coalesced into more formal categories of information. At a theoretical level this being 'formal', as distinguished from some suggested 'objective', knowledge – which is in practice 'objectified' by convention rather than as if some unique mode of knowing.

Reality can best be understood within a bio-evolutionary become civil-life perspective – think of all of the information that has been created and is being continuously added to – yes this would include all of the information entering the Universe since the beginning of time. Much of which, from a human perspective, can be dismissed as informational 'noise', of little lasting value, or is not detectable to our natural or even technologically aided, species informational band-width. But there remains a vast pool of more novel information – religious, historical, scientific, philosophical, cultural, artistic, wisdom, medical, agricultural, political, technological, communication, etc. – which is potentially available for us to access.

The information in forms of knowledge that we have access to is just that which has been recorded in some way, but also new information that is being produced as human life continues. Separating much of the 'noise' from the potentially more useful information can be a challenge. Any individual can only realistically access a tiny cross-section even of this potentially more useful Reality (as knowledge); the substantive constitution of her/his 'lived' reality. There is also all of the personal information related to a person's own experience including what

31

they know of their family, tribe, nation, past – the recorded and unrecorded biographies. The ways in which any of this information becomes known by individuals is liable to all of the limitations of human psychology such as bias, mistranslation, and ignorance (especially in terms of context) – it is an interpretive process with the associated fluidity.

Although I accept that this comment of possible bias, mistranslation, and ignorance, could be taken to imply some sense of an alternative 'truth', that there is some singularly authentic way of interpreting Reality, and of course I would reject this. Truth, as some pure concept (untainted by subjective considerations) is an inappropriate term by which to consider the informational content of Reality. It is just there, with humans themselves being tasked to assess the veracity of what they encounter, to reveal the intentional substrate of any particular piece of knowledge as a product. For example, the information relating to some historical conflict, technological innovation, or scientific discovery, can only have veracity when set in the wider context of current knowledge, if available, of the event; and/or by deploying hermeneutic devices deemed appropriate for understanding historically situated events as recorded by the participants and those enabling (as interpretation) the recording.

To repeat, I would distinguish two modes of Reality, epistemological and existential, 'every-thing' that is, and every relationship between things, all that can be thought whether possible or actual, is the collective psychological environment (milieu) of human-beings, past, present, and future. As well as this 'all' there is also the personal experience of each individual. A person can only gain access to but a relatively small cross-section of the 'all'. On both these modes of Reality, the collective and the individual, the boundaries are in a constant state of expansion. The sobering implication of this idea of our relationship to (or rather within) Reality being that we can only make judgements on a partial, provisional, basis. If for the most part this means a level of ignorance that we can assume is acceptable, both pragmatically and even epistemologically, in most contexts. But it is a deficiency that can assume the highest priority in seriously contested social, ethical, and political, issues.

As a species, the continuous expansion of Reality is not in terms of our 'discovering' (revealing) some pre-existing information, it is due instead to an interactive creativity arising from humankind's species engagement; humankind itself generates much of the substance of Reality, if via processes circumscribed by the limitation of species experience. Although any individual's awareness of Reality (their own re-ality) is, given the vagaries of memory and the 'graceful degradation' of some aspects of cognitive ability of our brains as we age, liable to contraction in areas as well as the expansion occurring as we absorb new experiences and learn new knowledge. Within each mode (Reality/re-ality) there is both that which is known and that which is unknown but is experientially 'out-there' waiting to be absorbed into the known, to become part of (individual and collective) self-consciousness. Humankind's evolutionary, become social, become civil, development has unveiled the massive expansion in accessible Reality – our reflective modality and accumulative capacity has enabled the realization of a sustaining mode of Reality – as information became knowledge.

I have already outlined the idea that we access ('know of') the contents of Reality by processing information. Biologically information is that which is processed by any organism in interaction with-in its environment (Jakob von Uexküll's 'Umwelt', 1934). Most of the nutritional material absorbed from the environment contributes to sustaining organic life but does not inform understanding (as does knowledge), it is for humans an aspect of the 'informational noise' referred to above rather than information in the sense that I wish to focus on; even if the informational 'noise' being exchanged at the molecular level, most obviously with DNA and mRNA, could be significant in a different hermeneutic context.

Information processed within a physical environment would allow any organism to search for the nutritional material but that which is subsequently ingested is not the form of information I am focusing on. For the human organism information can become symbolic and meaningful, assuming structures semantically shaped by subjective conditions and social contexts. Accepting of course that, given similar sensory apparatus and cognitive processing capacity, there is an ever-present potential for communicative commonality as well as unique subjectivity. Both are equally of importance for human life, subjectivity would not be aware of itself (in a human sense) without commonality. Each person's life being the product of continuous negotiational interaction between the individual and the collective. Commonality is not synonymous with objectivity, if the latter can be a socially constructed aspect of the former.

So, as we move on to consider language, let's leave Reality suspended in a condition of dynamic if 'bounded' complexity, yet ever-increasing (for humankind as a whole), an incomplete totality beyond any individual's comprehensive understanding. Any informational entity is included in the human Reality with which we are confronted and within which we exist. But it also includes ourselves; we are it as also we are in it.

The experiential membrane between ourselves and the world that we experience through the medium of our senses, including that which becomes in consciousness, is a synthetic one, constructed by a process of linguistic abstraction at the behest of our individual centres of awareness. As soon as we experience the world linguistically it becomes 'other' and yet so does a part of ourselves. Language does not belong to us as do our feelings and emotions. It can arise out of these and in turn (paradoxically) can also influence their intensity or style of expression. Language has a public construction, we draw it into ourselves as we develop and it becomes a part of our mental-life, available for both thinking and communication. Our original experience of Reality is as a feeling of oneness within it (as baby/young child), but we do not reflect. We feel, and are primarily engaged in seeking satisfaction of mainly physiological demands. As we grow our linguistic fluency develops, contributing to the developmental process of our being prised apart from the original sense of intimate oneness. The quite fluid entities involved in our own developing re-ality coalesce into linguistic structures, however loose and informal these might be. The mind through which we are aware of our re-ality involves linguistically infused integrating structures for making sense of those aspects of Reality we encounter. We are aware of our own selves as an original experience, but the primary means of obtaining knowledge of it is via linguistic formulation and

34

representation. If we also have images coming before the mind as well as language, and each are infused with emotions.

We can only know Reality in linguistic terms (a 'knowing' that can be routinely returned to for further consideration and if necessary reformulation) however useful might images be. Images are experienced via some 'inner eye' and are felt by the emotions whereas language can have an affective link with our emotions and can also represent aspects of reality in a formed way, best represented as knowledge.

It is possible that even as adults we can have non-linguistic experience, most obviously when in meditation or other types of mystical states. But when in this condition we gain no knowledge of it - the 'World'. If meditation leads to any form of knowing it is a type of intuition immersed in our pre-linguistic 'interior life'. Meditative experience can perhaps prepare us for and enable us to gain self-knowing, but this as intuition rather than as knowledge which by definition is communicable.

Knowledge that explains, describes, or analyses aspects of Reality and is communicable, can only be formulated in linguistic forms (Henri Bergson, notes language as 'fixing' Reality). I accept we could here enter into an esoteric discussion of intuition and pre-linguistic understanding; the latter occurring especially in inter-personal communication. And how language can connect to 'body language' incorporating the use of eyes, hands, the set of lips and similar linguistic 'shortcuts' (helping to reduce the 'semantic redundancy' inherent in any language), and other 'signals' such as, knowing grunts, worldly sighs, 'ums' and 'arrs'. Language is rarely, if ever, presented to the mind, even in the most sophisticated scientific treatise, in some perfect once and for all form; if certain forms of logical notation aspire to be such. Indeed, we often repeatedly rehearse and adjust what we are going to say or what we might have said. Any inner thinking or outer communication, even at the point of completion, becomes immediately liable to differing interpretation by self or others. At its most obvious, just consider how certain religious texts, with learned priestly castes determined to protect and circumscribe their meaning, still get interpreted differently as shifting human motivational and other intentional factors bear on the presented messages. According to Steven Pinker (1994, p237) "Words have stable meanings, linked to them by arbitrary conventions". And conventions are liable to differ between groups, and within a group, over time.

But I do not wish to become bogged down in all the implications the possession of linguistic ability has for humankind. I am seeking here, in a relatively un-contentious way, merely to differentiate between the knowledge that leads to effective understanding of the human condition and our personal lives, and some other forms that awareness takes. This in order to more closely focus on the medium through which we gain knowledge of the shifting complexity of our own segment of Reality. And as knowledge is represented to us in linguistic terms we need to consider the affect that language itself can have on our understanding, and so on our behaviour. I come back to other aspects of awareness when I seek to re-unite Reality, Language, and Thought.

It is sufficient to note here that language - both the 'inner' of thought, and the 'outer' of communication - is pervasive in effect and elusive in its nature. This source of indeterminacy might reflect the fact that human language is the 'growth-bud' continually re-interpreting our understanding of Reality; potentially enhancing our species adaptive response to its experience.

There is no comprehensive definition of language able to encompass all that its possession by humankind implies. It only becomes definable by emphasizing one or a few of its primary aspects whilst subordinating others; reflecting the multifaceted implications that its possession implies. Attempts at comprehensive definition have been more a reflection of the actual use the definer intends to apply it to. Recognizing this, I should like to develop my own provisional definition for the particular purpose of concentrating our attention upon how language use affects:

a) The way a person 'thinks' - that is the way she/he structures and conceives their uniquely personal cross-section of Reality i.e. their experience (intra-personal communication).

36

b) A person (or group's) relationship to others (inter-personal communication) and the negotiations and judgments they make about any area of the world that he/she shares with others.

These two areas in which language use play such an important role have implications. The first on the structure and content of thought which underlies and influences the way any person acts on-the-world, the second on how a person lives in-the-world with others.

Earlier I put forward a key characteristic for language, that it is 'synthetic'. In any linguistic experience we fix (synthesize) aspects of Reality which are re-presented in particular ways. The information coming before attention is poured into the mould of language, but in the process of formation its own structural characteristics (and the intentionality of the users/hearers) can contribute to shaping the mould. That which is represented to the mind has invoked the inter-relationship of both Reality and Language. Reality infuses our lives, we have a sense of duration and spatiality and can easily slip back and forth across the complex chronography and topography of each of these; accessing an 'information pool' of potentially infinite complexity. Language reduces this information (to facilitate adaptive understanding), as it assists the necessary editing process, to a more linear form; so being aligned with the basic structure of consciousness. Linguistic statements in themselves go from beginning to end in order to convey their meaning. Although, even as a statement is being made (remember this can be internally within a mind and also in inter-personal communication), other meaning streams can strike off to develop on their own.

I realize that I am in danger of compounding confusion, instead of promoting enlightenment, as I probe language from novel positions. At the risk of further compounding confusion, I offer yet another way in which language influences the information that comes before the mind (for us to make decisions about and/or to inform us), this is what I term the 'template effect'. In chemical engineering a template is a form or pattern that can serve to generate certain molecules (as DNA generates macromolecules such as mRNA); once the template is made this can have a determining effect on the item being engineered – I mean here to highlight the 'coercive' characteristics of language, most obvious in the nature of the syntax rules of grammar but also a form of more cognitive coercion circumscribing how any passage (narrative) can progress. Similarly, if usually (but not always, and sometimes dangerously so) in a somewhat less deterministic way, with language as you start on any 'statement' (again in- or ex-ternally) the lexical knowledge of the user, the syntactical rules of the particular language, along with the semantic (personal or social) context within which the statement is made, combine to influence the development of any statement. In other words, as a statement develops, whether a sentence, an essay, a speech, or a book, it becomes increasingly committed to take certain linguistic forms.

Such is the power of the human mind that we can, to a degree, overcome this tendency when we think it is operating against our more specific intentions. Edward De Bono, interested in the operation of intelligence, invoked the idea of 'lateral thinking' as a defence against the narrowing of our focus when using language in thinking. This type of (observer observing) approach will also serve to offset the linguistic 'template effect' which tends towards narrowing our focus. For our future this implication of language in use, if more flexible than a template as deployed in chemical engineering, is of fundamental relevance, touching centrally on political, ethical, and religious areas of existence.

Hans-George Gadamer posed the questions ('Truth and the Mind' - see supplement II): 'To what extent does language perform thought' – to what extent are there - 'preformed schemes of discourse'

His own answer being: '.....you must realize that when you take a word in your mouth, you have not taken up some arbitrary tool which can be thrown in a corner if it doesn't do the job, but you are committed to a line of thought that comes from afar and reaches beyond you.' He adds 'We speak that word and it leads to consequences and ends we had not perhaps conceived of.'

Three possible aspects of the 'template effect':

a) Conventional: as in the framework of syntax, and the assumed meaning of words and phrases.

b) The immediate social-cultural context within which a language is expressed, the influence of a sense of presence – the contextual milieu.

c) The realised accretions of experience as a sustaining influence on the intentionality of agents involved in any language situation; speaker/hearers, authors/readers

So language in itself contributes, has an intrinsic shaping effect, to what is produced and of course any linguistic production remains liable to variable interpretation. This is not to suggest that language is somehow separate from ourselves – we are truly 'language animals' – without it we would be but inarticulate creatures immersed in sensory information and emotional states. Language offers novel dimensions to our conscious lives, ones of articulate interpretation and cognitive understanding. Even accepting that our pre-linguistic 'immersion in sensory information and emotional states' continues as an enduring psychological presence.

In continuing to expose the synthetic characteristic of language, we can consider any event and, depending on our level of linguistic ability and our intentions, statements made about it are relative to these. But the same event can be interpreted or described in many differing linguistic formulations, some of which might be contradictory. These interpretations and descriptions are also relative to the time they are being made, a key aspect of context. Just to also note that language is even part of the perceptual mechanism that is first applied to events, so any representation is from the initial moments experienced in a way influenced by our linguistic background.

Language is flexible in application but once applied aspects of its synthetic character operate and statements tend to solidify, although the meaning of statements are never fixed (if the range of possible meanings can become narrowed) what is meant has achieved a form of semantic solidity. The synthetic characteristic of language is useful both in functional and existential terms. Without it the complexity of the Reality we access would slip and slide across our awareness, we would experience the colours, textures, and shapes (just as animals do in a more functional adaptive way), but not the human meaning of our experiences, we would feel but not know. It is a characteristic of language to fix the 'stream of consciousness' (William James), to structure information in forms we can use to understand, describe, and more generally conceptually access Reality.

As already noted, nothing I write about language need be taken to mean a separation between human-beings and language. We cannot be ourselves without it, we are so intertwined with language that it could be taken to be the one feature that most defines us as a species - Humankind, the 'Language Animal'. Its possession affects the ways we can perceive and conceive Reality, it allows experience to be represented and re-presented.

What are the further implications of the synthetic characteristics of the language faculty? Generally speaking, we can proceed through our lives without bothering too much with the effects outlined above. But when any description or interpretation is contentious, between individuals or groups, or when an individual is confused or doubtful about their thoughts, then a more careful consideration becomes necessary. We must be prepared to reformulate issues in ways that are hopefully more authentic in the way they seek to represent contentious events. All we know about language warns us that communication can be far from simple, especially when it comes to international political relations (and inter-ethnic conflict), and we need to be wary of assuming that any linguistic description or explanation can give a complete account of any situation.

As Aldous Huxley ('Essay on the Human Situation', 1959) noted:

'Language is what makes us human. Unfortunately, it is also what makes us too human. It is on the one hand the mother of science and philosophy, and on the other it begets every kind of superstition and prejudice and madness. It helps us and it destroys us; it makes civilization possible, and it also produces

those frightful conflicts which wreck civilization.'

Even on a personal level we can be aware of dissonance between thought and language. Once expressed language maintains its own semiotic existence. I cannot easily get beyond the 'already said', the 'already written'. I can but collate what I know of this as I feel it best relates to understanding or to explaining a particular issue. My attempts at these are often felt to be inadequate. I am uneasy with an articulation, the sense I wanted to convey has been eluded. I have learned to be satisfied with the acceptable (as some natural process of personal accommodation), to beware of 'over-thinking' - and only to attempt to reformulate if challenged. Just occasionally, I do feel that an expression does achieve an 'adequate grip' on conveying intended meaning – I can experience a sense of mental repose. In producing the linguistic expression I can realize the meaning in both the mundane sense of its formulation but also in the sense of actually refining or even completing the creation of meaning. The cruder pre-linguistic (inarticulate) thought pattern has been nicely polished (so articulated) in expression.

Language has enabled human-beings to experience existence at a richer level, in terms of conceptual material, than can any animal species lacking this facility. Without language (as a complex meaning-rich symbol system) we would have had no science, no religion, no philosophy, no society, no wisdom, and no literature, to mention just six areas. And in the last we see writers pursuing the possibilities of what language might be capable of. The descriptive brilliance of Charles Dickens or Leo Tolstoy, the intuitive understanding of human psychology sublimely expressed by William Shakespeare and Fyodor Dostoyevsky, and more naturally expressed by Thomas Hardy, Gabriel Garcia Márquez, Charlotte Bronte, George Eliot, Arundhati Roy, and John Steinbeck. The humour of a Saul Bellow or Miguel de Cervantes. The heightened, sometimes free-flying, imaginative work of James Joyce, Can Xue, Gunter Grass, Jorge Louis Borges, and Umberto Eco. The ability to show how social forces operate to influence world events, as carried out so well in the book 'Why we are in Vietnam' by Norman Mailer, the illuminating perception of evil in Albert Camus 'The Plague',

Ma Jian's 'Beijing Coma', or Victor Hugo 'Les Miserables', and the well-drawn vignettes on the human predicament in J.P.Sartre's 'Iron in the Soul' (the third book in a trilogy) and H.G.Wells's 'The Undying Fire'. To mention just a few examples of the power of language to enhance our experience of life; and these clearly exposing my literary limitations with its primarily male and more obviously 'Western' bias. The joyful literary freedom deployed by authors to explore the infinite possibilities inherent in language to express insights into our human nature and the psychological, social, and political forces within which it operates.

The interpretation of Reality aided by language enables us to gain the form of information as 'knowledge' denied to all other known organisms. It generally assists a person to arrange often complex lives, and in the products of the very best writers it exposes us to sublime forms of knowing. As both individuals and as a species it gives us a knowledge that can enable control, and so enhance our adaptive ability. And yet, in giving access to the higher level of consciousness, that of developed self-consciousness, we are cleaved from nature, cast into psychologically dark uncertainty from the comfort of the circumscribed worlds inhabited by other animals, young children, and certain types of 'primitive peoples'. If, for this last grouping, circumscribed by lack of access to knowledge rather than any lack of intelligence. Language and the (anxiety prone) cognitive mind-set it articulates, make us, as a species, the 'Cosmic Orphan' written of so eloquently by Loren Eiseley. Cast out by its linguistically articulated self-consciousness to wander forever with-in a Reality of ever-shifting meanings and a pervasive level of uncertainty.

Abstract language, in interaction with other aspects of cognition, has resulted in a separation from the natural world. Its rhythms and cycles, of living within a predictable conscious structure, an existential cocoon without much if any conception of a world beyond that bounded by comforting psychological and social horizons – the regularity and assumed predictability of the pre-linguistically lived.

For most social contexts our language encourages us to be

partial. It infuses statements with limitations as it informs and, in re-presenting Reality it in a sense divides us from ourselves. We process information, frame internal linguistic judgments, but whilst doing so we know that often from another perspective 'This is my view but if I were in his shoes' etc. we might well interpret what we take to be the same circumstances ('sign-situation') differently. But here we start to overlap into the next element of the Reality - Language - Thought triad as we begin to more obviously involve intentionality.

Just to begin to connect more directly with Thought, consider this simple example of the partial nature of linguistic statements, one not overly influenced by intentionality in a suspicious way, more just intentionality in relation either to knowledge of the subject matter and/or the purpose of making the statement. I am confronted with a large grey shape moving ponderously across my field of vision. I can say:

This is an elephant, an animal of interest to tourists due to its novelty interest - a sight to be seen in the wild.

or This is an elephant which is a patchedermal quadruped of the species Loxodonta africana, as studied by zoologists.

or This is an elephant, which the natives of this district can hunt down and use to feed themselves for a considerable period.

or This is a creature of monetary value of interest to ivory poachers.

All four statements could be valid but they contain considerably different amounts and types of 'overt' information and represent four differing perspectives framed according to intentionality.

In relation to pursuing the quest of outlining the source of evil in human life we can provisionally state that the 'down-side' to the possession of language is that its synthetic characteristic and the partial nature of any statement, along with its potential psychological power, make it liable to innocent misunderstandings and inadvertent misuse, but also amenable to the aims of the maladjusted, and the self-seeking - personalities, groups, or governments - to use for inhuman ends. And even for individuals more generally, the synthetic nature of language can cause confusion. We must always be aware of the fact that language (as spoken and written) is obviously a 're-presentation' (a form of interpretation) of experience not the experience itself; in this sense it is in fact a new way of experiencing any original generative experience (as Aristotle: suggested: 'Speech is the representation of the experience of the mind'). Although, as seen above, the form of re-presentation can impact as any issue develops, this being the internally generated influence on forms of linguistic representation; an element of the 'template effect' noted earlier. Any authentic re-presentation can be an elusive achievement, especially regarding contentious areas of experience.

Just as with Reality, let's leave Language as ambiguously outlined, suspended between its position of immeasurable value to our species in opening up our consciousness to forms of self-consciousness that enable us to process information in a way that no other species on Earth can. In earthly terms, placing us at the forefront of evolution, if assuming that evolutionary progress is a measure of the level of consciousness obtained. And the view that its synthetic characteristic divides us from the certainties of our organic selves. Such as experienced in the more confident unselfconscious sense of being-in-the-world which everyday humankind seems to strive to attain.

If Reality and Language are concepts that are difficult to grasp in terms of their essential implications then Thought is considerably more so; not least due to the other two being subsumed within it. This third concept in the triadic relationship posited has been termed an 'epiphenomenon' of the functioning brain, a type of potentially dysfunctional surfeit of activity of the neural system, a form of runaway externality of the brain's primary function of more instrumental adaptation to habitats. For Robert Ornstein this being brought about by the exceptional evolution of a particular organ (the brain). Ornstein has consciousness as an outcome of initially upright walking leading to an over-exuberant growth of the brain and so an excess of uncommitted brain cells.

Ornstein (1991, p65) set out this process as:

'The progression is stand up = > heat stress on the brain = > radiator for cooling = > changes in blood flow to the brain = > larger brain to provide extra, redundant cells = > uncommitted cells in the brain = > brain which could be used for other purposes not foreseen, as far along as is opera, science, metal sculpture, microchips, and marketing plans.'

But whilst such ideas, if arguably, might be of some explanatory value they do not help us to understand the implication of self-consciousness; the why as well as ideas such as Ornstein and others as to the how. I would suggest that an evolutionary theory based on increasing information-processing capacity as the primary driver of adaptation allows us to better understand humankind's place in the evolutionary development of life and its future direction post self-consciousness. And what Ornstein notes as the 'over-exuberant' growth of the human brain (and nervous system more generally) is consistent with this.

What we know as human thought is again, as with the substance of Reality, about information. Here it is not simply neutral information 'existing' out-there as potentially available for thought, but it is information in the state (condition) of being processed, so as 'intentionalized'.

In an abstract sense, what streams before the mind when thinking are images and forms of internal 'language', suffused in varying degrees by feelings and emotions. All of which are rarely fully formed but more-often have vibrational semantic boundaries which overlap and blend into each other. Thought is fluid and yet it is a fluidity punctuated with patterns of relative fixity – ones most obviously experienced when we come to a view, make a decision, or form a judgment. Thought comes in different forms within a variability related to intensity of attention: the generally relaxed type as when say driving a car and musing over one's own daily life, then there is the intensely focused type as when a surgeon is concentrating at a delicate point in an operation she attempts to clear her mind of all but the task immediately in hand, there is the intensely emotional type of thinking when engaged in a heated argument with a partner, or on a subject one feels passionate about, there is the type of thought as that undertaken by an air traffic controller during an emergency when a mental balancing act is attempted as incoming airplanes are stacked up and a landing slot is urgently sought for one which is damaged; priorities being decided against a background of lives in danger.

These are not distinct categories of thought, just simple examples to show the range and variety of attention-dependant thinking processes, and it is notable how easily we can switch from one type of thinking to another. The relaxed motorist can immediately switch from driving on automatic pilot, with the mind musing lightly on daily life or a radio commentary, to focused concentration when the brake-lights of the vehicle in front come on unexpectedly. It is as if the mind is designed to sort out priorities, and react accordingly, from amongst the varied information that comes before attention in relation to protecting an individual's well-being, or furthering their intentions.

As well as the informational material that comes before the mind we have evidence suggesting that there is a vast pool of unconscious material that whilst often not progressing into consciousness can influence the material that does. Between the unconscious and the conscious there is a mode of thinking we might term the preconscious, one that has perhaps lacked the attention applied to the other two. Possibly being less easy to delineate, and prone to express less easily described 'dispositional' influences. And yet it is a mode that is infused with an emotional form of intentionality that is of formative relevance to thinking, whilst also serving as a selective channel for memory (retention and retrieval).

There is even a sense of one's general intentional outlook being formed by the accretion of experience over a lifetime, forming a mode of pre-conscious (subliminal - preformed) intentionality. This material and its effects escape any clear delineation. But research in cognitive psychology has enabled a better understanding of the pre - and un - conscious material that is at least potentially available to consciousness.

A fairly simple description of the structure of the mind involves three features. That which comprises the material which is currently before the mind, and then a deeper intentional terrain involving purposes, judgments, willing, feelings, at a preconscious level, and also that deep, deep, pool of material which has accrued in the unconscious – material that can inform and influence pre-conscious and conscious thinking. I suspect that much of this deep-seated psychological material is in the form of emotions and feelings, becoming manifest in thought in more linguistic formulations. But the unconscious also includes that vast store of factual information – involving such informational content as all that which an individual has learned - in sum a store of knowledge as well as a person's more biographical information. We can also distinguish two types of (interconnected) memory – the recalled, re-interpreted, psychological material that we feel as incorporating our personal selves.

Firstly, a long-term memory (LTM) that includes all of the encoded information about past experience that can potentially be recalled; although recall is itself a variable ability. Sometimes the most complicated material can easily be recalled, at others a name one ought to know, it's on the 'tip of the tongue', remains inaccessible. Then a day or so later, when one thinking is in a relatively neutral mode, the name pops seemingly unsought into awareness. The variability of longer-term memory is now recognized for example in police work. When witnesses seem unable to recall significant aspects of a scene of crime investigators use a technique called the 'cognitive interview' which involves the witness being asked to visualize the crime from different angles, to try to remember what they were thinking just prior to coming to the scene, to express their feelings as they saw the crime proceed, to imagine themselves in the place of the criminal, the victim, or another witness. The main intention being to try to create different 'cognitive pathways' into the memory. This approach can sometimes retrieve a great deal of information that was inaccessible when the witness was simply asked to try as hard as they could to remember the scene. Research into the operation of long-term memory is casting considerable light on the ways in which awareness itself works (the dynamic 'in-presence' of consciousness). The second type of memory is termed short-term, or working, memory (STM), this includes all information from the LTM that is currently active before the mind and also remembering that which is just passing out of immediate attention but is still related to it, mostly remaining fairly easily accessible. This LTM/STM distinction is liable to simplify a complex, dynamic, set of interlinked activation processes, the operation of which we really only partially understand – I merely pose it as a descriptive working model that offers at least some sense of 'recall', a key element of both interpretation and representation. Consciousness is generally quite pragmatic in processing our experience in ways that allow assimilation within previously encoded meaning structures (similar to the 'schemas' of schema theory initially set out by F.C Bartlett, 1921) - if these being ever liable to renegotiation and adjustment – and/or ways that it can be accommodated to previous experience.

We identify that the central organ of thinking is the brain. Although writers such as Maurice Merleau-Ponty have with some literary style highlighted the involvement of the physical body as mediating between the mind and the world and the affect of this physicality – indeed an embodied pre-experiential sense of directedness towards the world. One of the basic assumptions I made when introducing this essay is that human beings have evolved from evermore primitive life-forms that can be traced as one looks back down the evolutionary trail. A distinctive feature of evolution being the development within organisms of a nervous system operating as a form of adaptational bio-mechanism. Initially more noticeable with the appearance of a primitive notochord, then with the progressive swelling of the anterior end of this into a bundle of nerve cells that coordinate the activity of the nervous (information processing) system running throughout an organism.

Very crudely put: with the reptiles a discrete nervous system co-ordinating region/organ ('proto-brain') becomes more obvious, overlying this (if reactively and proactively interconnected) the mammalian brain developed, then beginning about 30 m.y.b.p. the primate brain. Each new type (or mode – in relation to information processing characteristics) of the nervous system's central co-coordinating organ retaining similar functional features of those that preceded it; indeed being enmeshed with these.[5] In biological species terms, the most recent evolutionary development being the neurally complicated, folded, creamy-grey mass of interconnected cells, which is the human brain.

Usually with specific organs there is a species-common identity. If we accept the uniqueness of each person's immune system, one can say that one human kidney, heart, liver, spleen, etc. is much the same as another. They can be transplanted from one body to another and continue to function as previously; if allowing the need for immune-suppressant drugs to overcome the tendency toward rejection. With the brain, it might be feasible in some futuristic medical situation that transplantation could take place. However the effects of this (in anything other than perhaps a very young child) would have a dramatic impact on the person into whom the brain of another is transplanted. The whole mental contents, memories, feelings, body-related spatial awareness, emotions, intellectual ability, etc. would be markedly different, to the extent that the recipient would have a different identity. Imagine the transplantation of any other organ, the person would retain the same basic identity (if no-doubt somewhat altered from the experience of a significant medical intervention), but the contents of the brain, being unique to any individual, has an accretion of past experiences subsumed within an 'I' we term the identity of the donor. Why is this? Of what significance is this to an understanding of thought? To answer these two questions simply: firstly the very physiological construction (primarily the neural 'wiring') of each person's brain is unique, even for identical twins – each human brain contains about 100 billion neurons and about 1 million billion connections, or synapses. Each neuron can have from 100s to 1000s of direct connections to other neurons, with uniquely

---

[5] It would be misleading to consider this development as reflecting the triune-brain theory suggested by Paul MacLean ('*The paranoid streak in man*', 1969) which suggest a more discrete separation between the three stages of neural development; the dysfunctional interaction of these potentially leading to pathological outcomes. A key weakness with MacLean's view being, that there are identifiable homologues of each of the broad information processing modes (reptile, mammal, primate) within each preceding type of organism (see Fitch, 2010).

complex networks being formed during development by conditions set by the interaction of genetic constitution and lived experience, the result being a unique network of neural connectivity for each individual. And this has not even considered differences in other areas of brain function such as blood flow and other aspects of fine-grained electro-chemical constitution being different for each individual. The exact links between brain physiology and differences in individual human psychology are unclear but one suspects that there would be some relationship – shown most obviously with pathological conditions.

The basis for individual difference in physiological and other more experiential elements is a significant aspect of the human condition in that most of our understanding, as both individuals and in groups, is based on the pragmatically necessary assumption that we think in the same way, that our mental outlooks are similar. That anyone who 'thinks differently' could not only be wrong, or in our view misunderstand a situation, but that the difference could even be pathological and in need of treatment. Treatment which might be punitive (as in criminal) or more therapeutically intended to achieve 'normal' functioning (as in medical). The type of treatment applied depending on any prevailing socio/political ideological or medical model.[6]

This approach works in a general way, indeed life would be very complicated if we did not make such assumptions but, as mentioned above with language, when a contentious issue arises in interpersonal, inter-group, or international relations, it is of fundamental importance to reconsider the issue in the context of the potential diversity of the understanding of those directly involved in any issue.

Reference to the various formative experiences occurring during the 3,500,000,000 years plus of the evolution of life leading to the most complicated information processing bio-

---

[6] I feel the need to reinforce this comment in that any assessment of 'normal' can be contested, And having pathological conditions only focused on the individual might be misleading in that, seemingly pathological behaviours can more fairly be judged as a 'normal' reaction to adverse social conditions – especially during situations of military conflict, social oppression, and economic exploitation.

mechanism to appear in the known Universe can inform understanding of how it operates today. Aspects of thinking involving - motivation, judgments, willing, expectations, and similar can be better understood at the basic evolutionary level of adaptation to environments. But to gain a more comprehensive picture we must also consider the higher evolutionary level of human involvement in developed societies, where the mental 'forces' of the basic adaptive level are sublimated as they become less socially useful or even acceptable. We can philosophize by deploying highly abstract concepts that seem unrelated to our evolutionary heritage and how it infuses the ways in which we think. But without some grasp of the bio/evolutionary perspective we can rarely convincingly outline human thought processes – a necessary context within which to locate metaphysics. I do not claim that the science of socio-biology is the only approach to understanding the psychological aspects of the human condition; human life has developed within a complex nexus of societal relativities as the socio-cultural development continues to overlie biological evolution. I would only suggest that the biological evolutionary perspective, the way the central and peripheral nervous systems have been formed by a process of 'selective adaptation', can inform us about the possible causes of certain functional and dysfunctional aspects of personal and social human life and also provide illuminating insights as to the possibilities for our further psychological development, both as individuals and as a species.

Now I come to the nub of what I wish to focus on in relation to Thought. All we know about the thinking processes and the physiology of the primary organ by which they operate shows how subjective is human thought. Yes, there are similarities shared by individuals, and such aspects of thought as intellectual capability are confined within ranges of ability and aptitude. But the clear outcome of any rigorous study of thought shows its subjective base with always present the possibility of originality of expression and of interpretation. We 'reach out' to interpret behaviours, and to communicate with those who are experienced in their otherness. The extent of the necessary reaching out being primarily dependent on the closeness of the enculturalization experienced by interacting agents, as well as their dispositional and circumstantial intentionality.

Because of our potential for subjective originality we, as individuals, always have the potential to transcend the socially relative. From the mindless commitment to nationalism, or religious dogmatism, or simply obediently accepting the assumed normative expectations and claimed truths of any home society. But with our propensity towards intellectual torpor we rarely attempt to impose any fundamental originality on our lives, we tend to easily accept what we learn from others and the socialized interpretive frameworks through which we engage within experience, rather than create ourselves from the originating possibilities.

Subjectively is an experiential fact (a psychological element of Thomas Nagel's, 1974, 'What it's like to be human.....' or indeed for Nagel, a 'bat'), yet as soon as our thought moves beyond this primary reflection the limitations of focusing on subjectivity immediately become apparent. We confront the social in the everyday, but also as an accumulation of assimilations and accommodations integral to our past experience. An overemphasis on subjectivity leads only to a partial and limited analysis. To overcome these limitations the 'phenomenon' itself becomes the object of analysis, as it displaces but subsumes the subjective and the social. The nature of being human is that we are involved in a continuous process of negotiation between the individual (the self) and our assumed expectations of the social (the other/s).

Our social experience suggests to us that we can have a level of confidence in certain types of knowledge about Reality. For me it would be scientific knowledge, although I do accept what seems to be an intractable ontological limitation with this. And confidence in the reliability of scientific knowledge must be tempered by acknowledging the primacy of subjectivity, even accepting that scientific subjectivity can be subjected to critical and ongoing peer-group evaluation. Hence, providing that we understand the severe epistemological limitations of the phrase we can posit such an idea as that of 'objective knowledge'; perhaps better noted as 'scientific truth'. All 'objective knowledge' has an originating subjectivity, an existential fact that identifies an enduring epistemological fault-line. This is a primary reason why scientific knowledge is never fixed but progresses in whatever direction the interacting subjectivity's of scientific curiosity are focused on. If obviously, the current state of each science is also of relevance, even to the extent of influencing the research choices being made.

I wish to apply this positing of the primacy of subjectivity for thought to an idea noted earlier. I gave Thought a defining characteristic that of 'intentionality'. Within the emotional and conceptual material that streams before the mind we have experience of 'things'. From all the possible information-laden material that is available (seemingly 'out-there') we experience some things rather than others and these in certain forms. Certain features of these objects mean that we cannot experience the external world (or the information recalled from memory) 'willy-nilly', in accordance with some sort of internally generated motivations. What we experience is the outcome of an interaction between the world as it is and ourselves as we are (at any point in time). In philosophy the phenomenological approach is one that has endeavoured to take this complex ambiguity into account. Although even with such a profound phenomenological thinker as Edmund Husserl, the lack of any significant evolutionary perspective reduces the value of his conclusions. I accept that within the 'epoche' (a key aspect of Husserl's methodologically supposed pre-suppositionless 'bracketing') there is at least some potential to include evolutionary implications, but Husserl did not do so. His own concept of intentionality included historical factors but not evolution, indeed he expressed a certain intellectual antipathy towards (the dehumanising tendency of) modern science c. 1900-30.

Ever attempting to convey the intuitive authenticity of experience we must admit that most experience is of a dichotomy between ourselves 'in-here' and a world 'out-there'. As soon as we try to analyze this dichotomy beyond the simple immediacy of experience we have no way of assigning what aspects of any experience relate only to the in-here or only to the out-there. Each merges into the other, each in a sense creates the other and in order to cleanse our intellect we must admit that any experience is an amalgam of each, and so approach our analysis from the structure of the experience (phenomenon) itself without prejudging the internal/external balance of this amalgam. Seeking to follow the primary methodology of phenomenology but, contrary to this, deny the possibility of any pre-suppositionless beginning to analysis. This denial is in fact implicitly assumed within the phenomenology of Husserl himself, when he posits the intentional nature of all thought. Intentionality is not a neutral 'seeing of things' (as it was for Husserl's teacher Brentano) it is the active 'experience of things', thus acknowledging that we bring to experience an intentionality imbued with suppositions, some conscious some pre-conscious and some unconscious but affective. Merleau-Ponty recognized this when he wrote ('The Phenomenology of Perception', 1962, p136):

'......that the life of consciousness - cognitive life, the life of desire or perceptual life - is subtended by an 'intentional arc' which projects about us our past, our future, our human setting, our physical, ideological and moral situation, or rather which results in our being situated in all these respects. It is this intentional arc which brings about the unity of the senses, of intelligence, of sensibility and mobility.'

I would like to add the concept of 'intentional trove' – providing a sense of intentional resources as a life-long accumulation of directed experience indicating that intention in its immediacy is selected (consciously and unconsciously) from some 'store' in relation to biographical and situational elements of our experience. So 'arc' expresses the width (scope) of conscious intentionality and 'trove' expresses the depth (the pre- and un- conscious) of our intentional resources.

And it is this ever-present intentional arc/trove, in which inheres the accrued density of our experiences (for Merleau-Ponty both bodily and psychologically, the two being infused together) which negates any possibility of pre-suppositionless analysis. We can seek to minimize the influence of our intentionality but we can never escape its implications altogether.

Husserl's own intentional 'object' relates to a web of other connected intentional objects. For a simple example of this idea..... when we 'see' the front of a stationary car we also 'experience' the car in motion, the rear and side views etc. One intentional experience can potentially call-up numerous past experiences of similar objects. Thought, for Husserl, flows in an interrelated intentional way.

Husserl's later outline of intentionality took two forms – the more standard 'phenomenological intentionality' which contributes to forming the pre-predication of the natural unity of experience and an 'operative intentionality' inherent in decision-making and judging. Merleau-Ponty follows Husserl's distinction but made much more of the operative, highlighting a continuous sense of bodily involvement ('body schema') as well as pre-conscious psychological sources. Primarily, but not only, this encompasses the constitution of the type of 'intentional arc' suggested by Merleau-Ponty. One that situates us within a range of relationships and the accrued experiences of our past lives, our plans for future projects, and our more ideological outlook.

My own concept of intentionality differs from those of more traditional (analytic and phenomenological) approaches. Very simply described: in phenomenology intentionality is centred on the unmediated relationship between subjectivity and the object (as phenomenon), and in analytic philosophy as the relationship between the thinking self and the 'external world', as mediated by language. Whereas my own concept centres on a more constituting, more dynamic 'what' of intentionality, rather than on the more placid content of it, as was the case with most phenomenological and analytic approaches. My interest is in intentionality as it is involved with interpreting experience, especially in relation to personal motivation and judgement.

G.E.M.Anscombe ('Intention', 1957) argued that intention is not related to the psychological process leading to an act or judgment but is a function of the type of questions that can be applied to acts or judgments. She suggests that an act can be intentional under some conditions but unintentional under others, in contradiction to my view that all acts have an intentional substrate. Anscombe gives the example of a motorist who, when asked why he was driving at sixty miles per hour, says that he was not conscious of going at that speed. An act that seems for her to be unrelated to any intention. I would reject Anscombe's view, she is taking a limited interpretation of intentionality. I suggest that a range of reasonable questions can be asked of any act or any judgment. The man driving the car presumably pressed down on the accelerator to the point where the vehicle exceeded sixty miles per hour. If we allow that he did so unintentionally (even if the passing scenery would have indicated quite rapid movement to him) and if he was to be involved in an accident, do we then accept a plea of his unintentionally travelling at sixty miles per hour because he was unaware of doing so. I suggest the driver might have been unaware of driving at sixty miles per hour but he did do it intentionally. It was merely an intention below the level of immediate consciousness as this spirals down into the pre- and sub-conscious intentional substrate.

I would also highlight the role of conscience in our thinking lives as a potentially key element of intentionality – sourced in our socialization processes (primarily based on family and social relationships) as these have interacted with our own developing individual intentional psychological resources. Our conscience, as with all identifiable elements of thinking, impacts differently on individuals and even on the same individual at different times – if accepting that for most there is a 'negotiable continuity' operating to guide how we assess issues and monitor our own behaviour. I suggest that the influence of conscience – a continually recursive process 'monitoring from within' has an as yet understated importance to our thinking (and so also behavioural) intentional selves.

Thinking is broadly a linear process (linked by duration) infused with almost continuous recursive reflection – restating, reinforcing, and rehearsing various elements of thinking.

W. James 'Principles of Psychology' 1891, pp233-4 noted that:

"Our state of mind is never precisely the same. Every thought we have of a given fact is strictly speaking, unique, and only bears a resemblance of kind with our other thoughts of the same fact........experience is remoulding us every moment, and our mental reaction on every given thing is really a resultant of our experience of the whole world up to that date."

Within this flowing process of developing ideas, the intensity and indeed the form of any experience is affected by the underlying intentional substratum. A substratum that is the accrued density of significant experiences developed throughout our lives. Intentionality is a primary driver of behaviour – and, by implication, a primary element in the expression of evil.

Now having prized three aspects of our mental life apart, in order to consider them (their interlinked triadic relationship) from the defining characteristic I gave each of them, I now return them to the unity which is their 'natural' experiential state.

Since we can now overcome the unhelpful subject/object (this is a primary insight of phenomenology) and the subject/social dichotomies when considering the material of experience, with a higher-level concept of 'phenomena' to bound what we feel as ourselves in-here and the world we feel as out-there within an existentially inextricable relationship, we can less self-consciously refer simply to 'that material which comes before the mind'. Even accepting that the concept of mind is itself rather nebulous, but that as a referent to some specific process and/or attribute it is perhaps seen as more adequate. I mean by mind that concept which represents the outcome of the psychological activities of thought and the physiological activity of the nervous system – contributing to experience realised in self-conscious awareness. It is not intended to be too ridged, and is only deployed as an 'entry concept' leading towards a finer-grained analysis. The mind is commonly assumed as being physically located in the brain (interconnected to a wider nervous system) but is more-often referenced as a seemingly non-material presence closely associated with our personal selves. It might help to compare mind with what is usually understood as the traditional 'I', with a sensed relationship to physiological connections spreading throughout a body's nervous system, each (the seemingly non-material and the seemingly material) blending in an affective relationship into the other.

That which comes before the mind (the mind includes the observing I, as a reflective presence rather than some form of 'homunculus') is a fluid amalgam of Reality - Language – Thought. Understanding this material requires a form of speculation unrelated to the idea of any ultimate truth. Put simply: in any particular situation information drawn from within Reality is structured according to linguistic frameworks in conformity with the psychological constitution (including the intentional requirements) of an individual.

A primary implication of my description of Reality is that whatever conclusions arrived at about human mental activity can only have a provisional type of truth (Socrates early on recognised the provisional status of knowledge). This is not to down-play what can be learned and what value it might have. Understanding, based on the consideration of available information, is probably the surest form of knowledge; be it scientific, religious, traditional wisdom, or other. The type of knowledge being arrived at following a thorough analysis of a situation, an analysis that includes examination of all possible facts that seem relevant, as well as an open examination of the 'intentional arc/trove' of the individual/s undertaking any analysis, including any practical or theoretical limitations arising from this. As already noted, in this speculative context, analysis is about constructing conceptual 'tools' designed and deployed to produce increased understanding of the human condition.

It is fairly clear from my outline of thinking that I view the phenomenological approach, radically modified by the infusion of an evolutionary perspective, and with the admission that all analysis from the start involves presuppositions, as the most useful philosophical base on which to found any analysis of particular situations. This approach implies that one should be led by the phenomena (situations) themselves, to not be limited by partial and/or otherwise distorting perspectives such as functional, behavioural, ideological, and similar potentially restrictive aspects of any phenomenon.

With the reservations made above, I consider this the most adequate way to approach my primary subject matter, which is human existential experience. The aim being to start with phenomena but seeking to bound any particular experience within a conceptual framework that has value only for analysis and is not in itself an explanation of the way we think.

Before outlining this framework I should like to take stock of what I am trying to achieve. I am trying to understand the human condition from the perspective that this condition is problematic, centering on the existence of 'evil' in human history. I have found human experience to be of variable interpretation, factors in a situation (phenomenon) that one individual emphasizes another ignores, another cannot even see, yet all potentially 'belong' to the experience. This can provide a basic explanation as to a possible source of much misunderstanding and conflict between individuals, groups, nations, etc. The implication being that ignorance is a cause of evil and that we mostly fail (intentionally or otherwise) to consider all the factors relevant to any situation; to look only for those corresponding to our own intentionality. Not realizing that these intentions might be flawed in that they could arise from a partial (or even misguided) understanding of the motives of others and of the constitution of experience. That a broader perspective on any phenomenon, gained from a more comprehensive understanding of it and how it relates to wider human reality, could at least offer the potential to enlighten, and thereby dispel, ignorance.

I should like now to present a key conceptual idea that is of central relevance to my analysis. I suggest it would be heuristically useful to view any phenomenon as a 'sign-situation'; the hyphen indicates 'signs' as being the primary meaning units of any 'situation'. Some general uses for signs are: A <u>sign</u> can point to something else, as a footprint would be a sign that a creature has passed by. A <u>sign</u> can serve as an instruction, prescriptive or prohibitive, such as 'drive on the right' or 'keep off the grass' notices. A <u>sign</u> can provide directions to a place such as Reasonville > 5kms. These show three different types of sign use. The first signifies something that is not present. The second an act to be undertaken or avoided. The third the direction and distance to a destination. As will be seen, these three general uses in their abstract rather than practical sense apply to my concept of 'sign-situation'. Sign here implies potential for meaning and situation implies experiential boundary – indicating the possible parameters that we can project around an issue to allow a clearer focus on it. Even accepting that these boundary conditions are porous, and across which information can seep - but there is more to my concept. There are similarities between my meaning of sign-situation and the concept of sign outlined at the beginning of Chapt.III 'Sign-Situations', in that classic book on the relation of language to thought, 'The Meaning of Meaning' by C.K.Ogden and

I.A.Richards (first pub.1923, 10th ed. 1972). But I would reject the combination of behaviourist/ associationist psychology underlying their analysis and the limited potential for their sign's development. Their sign-situation focuses on the more simple relationship of sign to referent (signified) but I am seeking to convey the idea of a sign-situation as circumscribing a potentially information-rich contextuality. So crudely put, Ogden and Richard's initial sign-situation but in a qualitatively more dynamic form. The two-part concept connects 'sign' with 'situation'. I mean to convey the union of 'sign', pointing to a significance which underlies any experience, with 'situation', that seeks to convey the way we ('we' in the sense of we-in-experience, a balance of subjectivity with-in Reality) psychologically 'bound' experience in order to gain understanding. In this sense it would be phenomenal, awaiting, more often anticipating, interrogation.

A 'sign-situation' would serve as a useful starting point to assess any particular experience, providing that in seeking clarity it is accepted that one must progress from the initial assessment into the originally experienced sign-situation and any others which might radiate from it, and if necessary (which it usually is) to also consider the generative, so genealogical, intentionality involved.

A comparative, if simple, analogy: a 'sign-situation' can be compared to a balloon, when deflated (an initial encounter) it can contain very little information but from which it can expand to encompass ever larger amount of inter-related information. In theory the sign-situation/balloon can expand indefinitely, because it is possible, at least in theory, to connect everything in Reality with everything else. But functional requirements (as well as more 'natural' cognitive processes), indeed the need often to come to some conclusion, means that any sign-situation based analysis has experiential limits; if metaphysical sign-situations invariably remain 'open,' and scientific ones are continuously engaged in a process of internal development.

Sign-situations can be usefully conceived as being the meaning-laden 'atomic' units that make up experience; or perhaps better expressed as the semantic quanta constituting the corpuscular continuum of experience. At their least significant, the signs within sign-situations are the minimum information packages that any experiential phenomenon can be reduced to. As more formal representations in language these signs could be the phonemes (42-44 in English), if as only single sound-related 'differences' within a language they would lack the significance of a sign in terms of meaning.

Sign-situations can coalesce together to form a sign-situation of higher order, constituted by increased information complexity. And, similar to the 'atoms' of modern physics, they can be reduced to 'internal sign-situations' when individual signs are being focused on.

As stated above, sign-situations are not in themselves conclusions/judgements, although they are conceptually the material source for these, they are not explanatory but rather they are descriptive. They describe the (phenomenal) structures of what we experience, in themselves, they cannot explain the meaning of any experience; even if any 'sign' in its immediacy is informed by meaning. The interpretation of the structural descriptions of sign-situations, in conjunction with the intentional context can, taken together, produce more useful explanatory conclusions.

Just as sign-situations can expand to encompass more information – as constructed to widen their contextual relevance – so too can any complex sign-situation be de-constructed, and a reductionist analysis can be undertaken if required. Bear in mind that this form of reduction can reveal that which has been concealed, as motivations, interpretive perspectives, or initially missed connections and implications.

But the potential meaning-scope of any sign-situation is never exhausted – experience involves the continuous interpretation of information streaming through the senses ('as if' externally generated) and information streaming within the mind ('as if' internally generated) - the circumscription of discrete sign-situations (more formally experienced as particular issues/events) is a primarily subjectively-generated (voluntarily and involuntarily) partial selection of information from the veritable stream, always there to be returned to.

From early in humankind's civil life some thinkers have seen explanatory value in positing 'atomic' entities as primary constituting units. They included the Greek philosophers Leucippus and Democritus (both flourished circa 440 - 420 BCE) and much later on, scientists such as Pierre Gassendi (1592-1655), Isaac Newton (1643-1727), and John Dalton (1766-1844) have seen a value in positing forms of atomic entities to underpin their more materialistic speculations. A tradition that sought clarity in reductionist starting points. Three philosophical thinkers: Gottfried Wilhelm Leibniz (1646-1716 C.E.), Alfred North-Whitehead (1861-1947), Arthur Koestler (1905-1983) have also contributed to this tendency towards atomic reductionism. To seek abstract grounds for forms of bottom-up analysis.

Leibniz's Monads, each one being an infinite number of un-extended substances (each monad being a soul). Monads do not interact in any causative way; they operate, for Leibniz in accordance with a god-given pre-established harmony. No two monads are alike. Monads are of different types forming a hierarchy of superiority '....in the different degrees of clearness and distinctness in the perception of their respective souls or dominant Monads...' (From Robert Latta's 1898 translation of: 'The Monadology', first pub. 1714, p1205). For Liebniz, the human body is composed of immortal monads, with a dominant monad constituting the soul of the person whose body it is a part of.

Whitehead's atomic 'actual entities' (populated by 'occasions') are quite extended abstractions. 'Actual entities', are the final real things of which the world is constituted. Processes involving what he terms 'prehensions' arise from the initial (subject based) analysis of actual entities. With this element of them (prehensions) providing the link between actual entities, so allowing the conditions for a unity of experience involving past, future and present experience (a 'unity of appropriation'). Such a grouping of actual entities is termed a nexus. A 'nexus', for Whitehead being 'actual entities' involved with each other by reason of their prehensions of each other. The ultimate facts of immediate experience are actual entities, prehensions, and nexus. All else is, for our experience, derivative from these. He also notes an ontological principle; that the reasons for things are always to be found in the composite nature of definite 'actual entities'.

Although Whitehead's actual entities are not atomic in the indivisible sense of classical physics they are atomic as in the modern model including, perhaps especially, quantum physics. If more processes (of overlapping 'occasions') than fixed models, actual entities are, for Whitehead, the fundamental constituents of our experience. (Whitehead, 'Process and Reality', 1929)

Koestler's 'Holon', is based on the view that the experience of 'objects for thought' (e.g. cells in a body, or a part of any discrete social institution) are arranged in hierarchies. Holons 'look' both ways, up and down any hierarchy (their being 'Janus' faced), forming parts or wholes depending on the perspective taken. Koestler's holons are far less abstract than Whitehead's 'entities' and less imaginative than Liebniz's 'monads', his being used to describe conventionally understood interconnections within biological and social hierarchies. (Koestler, 'Janus: A Summing Up', 1978)

Although my 'sign-situations' differ quite significantly from each of these (few parallels other than a general 'atomic' approach as an abstract idea) I consider myself in this tradition that appears on initial encounter as reductionist but, as reflection proceeds, can develop into fairly complex entities, offering quite wide descriptive scope. A tradition that favours a psychological propensity driven to begin analysis with simplification, a strategy that offers some sense of containment to the infinite eternity of the unmapped metaphysical terrain.

So, for heuristic purposes, I initially reduce the 'things' that emerge in thought during our be-ing-within-the-world to relatively bounded concepts termed sign-situations. But as soon as our conception moves beyond the recognition of a simple unity in experience the boundaries of sign-situations can start to overlap as they reconfigure into meaning-laden webs of connections to other sign-situations that can radiate from the immediate focus of thought. Progressing to form higher order signs-situations (more information-rich) to the point where they would be better considered as circumscribed events and issues; even as wars, scientific theories, and political ideologies.

Signs-situations, because they represent meanings, are ever-open to interpretive variation.

The philosopher Jacques Derrida's post-structuralist type of reconsideration of language suggests a serious difficulty not just in interpreting the ideas of others, but even in interpreting our own internally generated ideas. This being due to the interpretive fluidity that adheres to signs. For Derrida, with any sign there is always surplus of meaning. This extended potential for difference is inherent in any sign within a sign-situation. Difference as in a conventional, more static condition and also his own Différance deployed to indicate a sense of meaning deferred. A deferral that, if realised, can impact on any difference/s initially noted.

I posit the idea of 'sign' as representing a discrete component of our conceptual and perceptual experiences – any constituting sign manifests itself as meaning, in effect and affect the 'signified'. Some directive signs are relatively simple – no-entry, keep off the grass, drive on the left, etc - for these the interpretation of meaning is relatively straight-forward. But for other signs (ones infused with emotional capital) - a Nazi symbol, a Christian Cross, words such as freedom, duty, terrorist, nation, and similar 'hot' images and concepts – interpretation is more about the production of meaning and this as in how the higher-order sign-situations, such as the events and issues noted above can develop. How this development proceeds (its ongoing production) involves a set of elements. These being mostly related to the interpreter's own experience and the (conscious and unconscious) intentional approach they bring to any interpreting situation.

Signs can be seen as the sub-atomic units of perceptual/conceptual experience (the simplest perturbations in the discontinuous 'flow' of consciousness) but bear in mind even the simplest of signs can be irredeemable fluid in relation to meaning. Just consider the meaning of a Hammer and Sickle flag for a committed Bolshevik compared to that of a White Russian in the 1920s, or the initials IDF for a Jewish citizen of Israel compared to that of a Palestinian living in the West Bank in 2021.

This potential for fluidity (of differential interpretation)[7] of

---

[7] This fluidity can be both inter-personal.... a differential interpretation that individuals and groups are liable to, but this fluidity can also apply to a

meaning increases significantly when we consider aggregates of signs as sign-situations. Now the patterning of associated signs involves an increasingly wider range of contextual information. It is here in these more developed forms that we can investigate such sign-situations as represented in any 'discourse' – primarily in written and spoken language and in moving or fixed images, but sign-situations can also be a central aspect of internalized thinking processes. It is in this setting (discourse - involving signs and sign-situations) that we can interpret the articulation of our experiential lives.

In line with my ongoing analytic approach bear in mind that I posit 'signs' and 'sign-situations' as but heuristic devices designed to assist in understanding aspects of our lived experience. And indeed, I also assume this of the idea of 'discourse' – as but another concept useful for investigating motives and intentions behind the production and interpretation of information and indeed the relevance of the social context within which discourses are produced.

In this context I am acknowledging that such devices will no doubt be improved on in relation to purpose. My expectation is that using the cruder one that I posit will assist our understanding to the extent that we will learn how conceptual interpretative devices can be improved in design, in relation to purpose, as we advance our understanding of our be-ing in the world.

Moving more specifically from sign to sign-situation, and so to consider the processes involved in the information-enriched radiation from any initial encounter within some circumscribed pattern of information-content, the analysis of discourse can be relevant. Discourse analysis has come to be a specific investigative technique used in the social sciences of psychology, anthropology, sociology, and also in philosophy where it

---

single person being liable to differentially interpret the same (or very similar) issues and ideas. This last, whilst perhaps frustrating at times, provides the small chink of 'light' offering the potential of individuals to change attitudes and behaviours, if provided with new information, or if an issue can be re-interpreted – in humanistic terms this offers the potential for good if individuals can be persuaded (usually by dispelling ignorance) to more enlightened views.

overlaps with a more general hermeneutics.[8]

Discourse analysis is a technique of disclosure deployed in the study of a range of cultural artefacts. Given that intentionality always informs any discourse, these can be framed as products: ones constituted by an intermixing of signs linked by meanings, and the sign-situations in which these are connected and expressed. And when we consider this production as identified in areas such as the political, scientific, religious, educational, economic, and in interpersonal relationships, we can seek to highlight the use of 'power'; a key element of all socially situated discourse. Power is a concept of central relevance for understanding discourse production. The ability to persuade, dominate, cajole, force, manipulate, demand, 'nudge', and similar overt or covert means to influence the interpretation of any issue; this including how an issue is viewed from its initial presentation onwards. The power inherent in authority figures and institutional frameworks to even set the parameters of acceptable discourse, and so to be able to define and redefine meanings and to influence the assumed implications of these.

The use of power is most obvious when its deployment results in one or more people undertaking or believing something that they would not undertake or believe unless these had been presented in the context of power being deployed. But power can be willingly submitted to if we accept the authority of those wielding power, of those felt to be more knowledgeable than ourselves, those who we have been persuaded to believe to be contributing to progressing our own interests – or those who are generally 'taken for granted' as having more authority (authority, however gained, is a reservoir of power). These authorities would include those such as: parents, partners, priests, imams, tribal chiefs, rabbis, politicians, teachers, various types of expert, media commentators, and the wealthy (who gain

---

[8] For Wetherell, Taylor and Yates (Open University, 2001, 'A Reader', p1) 'Discourse analysis is concerned with the meaning that events and experiences hold for social actors. It offers new methods and techniques for the social researcher interested in meaning-making. More than this, however, discourse analysis is also a theory of language and communication, a perspective on social interaction and an approach to knowledge construction across history, societies and cultures.'

authority simply by their economic substance), and similar individuals who can operate in situations where the form of power dynamics are asymmetric (differential – as in economic, political, educational, psychological, and legal, contexts). In the UK this can also apply to institutions such as the NHS, and the BBC, and in certain contexts the government, where power is realised due to 'respect' accorded to these by a significant proportion of the population. But of course, power can also operate unconsciously when infused within the normality of any social context.

We all have some power (not a easily quantifiable entity - which can be of wisp-like elusiveness or of hammer-hard impact), the seemingly weakest of us have some, if marginal, capacity to rebel, or to bully those even more deficient in power.

The philosopher Roland Bathes also noted a quite subtle form of power that can be deployed in discourse as: 'I call discourse of power any discourse that engenders blame, hence guilt in its recipient.' (Barthes, 1977, cited in Kearney and Rainwater eds. 1996, p365). An observation that works well in capturing the essence of outcomes in certain affective (more interpersonal relationship) settings but is inadequate to express the multiplicity of the implications of power deployed wider than this to the types of power that engender significant behaviour and/or attitude change.

When discourse produced as texts, speeches, images, and film, is being analysed, certain interrogative questions can be usefully applied, ones such as: What is assumed (the normal, the taken for granted) - What is missing (other voices and facts) - What misleading or partial generalizations have been made – What are the formal and informal practices regulating any discourse - How and in whose interests has power been deployed within any discourse - Have misleading stereotypes or metaphors been noted – How has priority been accorded to certain concepts – e.g. freedom, the good, the bad, duty, The Party, national-interest, foreigner, terrorist, and similar potentially contested concepts - Have 'decoys' been inserted to mask possible implications of a claim or other aspects of a narrative e.g. 'Bankers' being blamed for a financial crisis to mask a systemic problem in the financial system itself, or the blaming of the whole German or Japanese nations in 1945 to mask a failure of international politics.

The insertion of 'coded' messages within any discourse can be difficult to identify as these are based on understandings known (initially) only by the composers and the intended recipients of the messages – the internet has proven to be especially amenable to such aspects of communication. A fairly obvious example being of a narrative thread within a discourse set in the political context of the USA circa Jan. 2021 repeating the theme of 'fighting for our freedom', a coded message that 'we' need to keep 'our' guns and to be suspicious of anyone who is not like 'us'.

Investigating the primary narrative themes of a piece of discourse can be simple, as in overt nationalist/racialist propaganda, of heroically presented images of dictators, or of crude advertisements. But in the discourse products of those such as skilled speechwriters, journalists, mendacious politicians, skilled advertising copywriters and biased historians, then the answer to analytic questions similar to those noted above more often have to be teased out. With the discourse having to be mined for seams of implication and these exposed to the light produced by forensic examination. The hidden needs to be articulated and its possible implications outlined. Discourse analysis is the investigative process of considering the implications of meaning as presentation, primarily as language in use but also for any type of sign-system.

The power of discourse can increase when discourses combine.....the power of a message repeated and of diverse forms of authority reinforcing a message. This accumulative power of discourse is of particular relevance to investigating ideologies, meta-theories, and the prevailing 'paradigms' such as those noted by Thomas Kuhn in science. What Michel Foucault noted as the 'episteme' (the discursive formation) in relation to the assumed to be set of authoritative knowledge related to a social practice (for Foucault: sexuality, the prison system, 'madness') at any location and historical period.

For Shani Orgad on discourse, with a focus on representations within the media: '.....on the one hand, representations are seen as open to multiple readings, inherently ambivalent, and constantly changing. On the other hand, representations are seen as 'dominant' 'preferred' meanings and carrying particular ideologies reinforcing specific ideas and values and excluding others, which works largely to reconstitute and sustain existing power relations.' (Orgad, 2012, p34)

The work of socially engaged philosophers – and those others who would pursue the study of signs and sign-situations (in effect the investigation of the implications of meaning) – is to be tasked with deconstructing discourse. To identify dominant narratives and so expose the conditions for these to be challenged. A process of revelation setting out from the more obvious questions: by whom, for whom, and why...... as these elements contribute towards the production of an identifiable narrative. Before then progressing to unpeel the layers of meaning and motivation inherent in any discourse.

The value in positing signs and their more dynamic development within sign-situations is that these provide a heuristic device that we can use to circumscribe a portion of our experience that can be sufficiently useful for analysis whilst acknowledging the fluidity in an ever-changing form of process conditionality. Lived reality subjects us to a continuous shower of what is experienced as externally generated information, along with what is experienced as internally generated emotional and more cognitive information, such that we would be overwhelmed if we could not process this in 'chunks', and signs set within sign-situations offer a flexible form of abstraction to cognitively manage this.

The simple unity of a sign-situation as it first arises immediately begins to change with the development of the thinking process. Let's try a very simple example: I see an object in the sky that I identify as an airplane in flight, a simple sign-situation. As the thinking process develops, and if the sign-situation stays in attention, it perhaps connects to a memory of another airplane I once flew in; the intentional (meaning-laden) radiation begins. I then think of the destination and of the attractive person I once met on a beach, the original sign-situation has overlapped into other ideas which can then be incorporated as aspects of the original sign-situation or can possess the possibility of becoming bounded sign-situations in their own right; which happens depends partly on those I pay attention to and partly on any interesting changes in the sign-situations themselves. For example: I might be so stimulated by the memory of the attractive person that my thought focuses closely on them (for a moment in thought the sign-situation boundary is experienced as relatively fixed – as I reflect more closely on the memory), the original sign-situation (airplane in the sky) has faded, even though I might still have it in view, into some semi-conscious background. Or, whilst making the attractive person connection, I notice black smoke start to stream from one of the engines of the airplane. This time the image of the person immediately disappears from thought and I am instead focusing intensely on the distressed aircraft. As my thinking radiates from this dramatic change in the original sign-situation thoughts about possible rescue arise in the mind, call the emergency services, wondering how many people are on board, and similar ideas that arise in disaster-related scenarios. I might even experience a frisson of empathic fear as I project myself into the place of a helpless passenger in the plane or a crew member in the emotionally intense atmosphere of the cockpit. So, the original type of encounter with any sign-situation is simply related to the focus of our attention (with its constituting intentionality), but when a sign-situation has been developed, it has accrued a mass of possible descriptions and meanings. And bear in mind that any sign-situation has the possibility of infinite complexity. Where we limit any sign-situation's developmental expansion depends on a number of factors. It might happen semi-consciously as a person's interest declines, or due to our having made a judgement we are satisfied with, or perhaps because we cannot obtain any new information.

Above I gave a simple example of a sign-situation as a developing process and I think I can expect that the heuristic use-value of a sign-situation can be seen. The use-value of this example is relatively limited, but consider the current conflicts continuing to rumble-on on the Middle East, more especially Palestine/Israel. I suggest the use-value of the sign-situation concept can provide descriptive, and so set the conditions for analytic, value here. It more easily allows an issue to be immediately circumscribed as 'problematic' rather than as a confrontation between two (or more) 'sides' – so a shared framework rather than one of isolated polarities. As a sign-situation the conflict is circumscribed so we can attempt to fairly precisely identify the views of those more directly involved, including the populations that any leaders purport to represent. Radiating from this are the historical implications and the often varying (contradictory) interpretations of historical 'facts' made by the antagonists. There are also the specific grievances, military resources, and external alliances, to be clearly outlined. Along with the challenge of identifying credible mid-long-term shared interests[9]. This all informing an assessment of possible ways of resolving or at least limiting the extent of any conflict.

The structure of the significant individuals' intentional perception (this could if necessary be a community's collective intentionality) of both the immediate sign-situation, and the more reflective higher-level sign-situation, needs to be understood by anyone wishing to clarify the conflict in terms of a possible negotiated resolution. Sign-situations are always a loosely bounded 'unity' within a process of their continuous development. Of fundamental importance is to place any conflict, the higher-level (more complex) multi-faceted sign-situation that would invariably radiate from the initial circumscribed sign-situation, within a wider 'World' context. A context that involves the question of how this particular conflict and suggested resolutions (or even just accommodations) relate to an assessment of how the 'World' itself is developing.

---

[9] There is also the critical question of each group's desired outcome; groups as in populations involved not the leaders, who might have a different intentional perspective – perhaps related to maintaining political power or economic and social privilege.

Chapter 2: The concept of 'meaning' within be-ing

I now wish to introduce something that has appeared in rather veiled (tacit) forms throughout this essay, if used so far in quite conventional ways. A conceptual something the reference to which lies at the very core of all our be-ing. The concept of 'meaning', a concept that has a bewildering range of uses, in sometimes markedly differing contexts (rather ambiguously meaning itself is polysemous): A red light on a set of traffic lights 'means' something to the motorist - We talk of 'the meaning of life' - In interpersonal communication we expect people to understand 'what we mean'. When a young man, the boxer Frank Bruno in radio or television interviews with the broadcaster Harry Carpenter used to follow almost all commentary statements with the semi-rhetorical question "You know what I 'mean' Harry?" – The philosopher C.E.M.Joad, as a member of the panel on the popular 1940s radio programme 'The Brains Trust', would often begin his response to a question from a member of the public with the statement 'It depends what you mean by......' in doing so acknowledging the variable nature of meaning. We talk of the 'meaning' of love, or the 'meaning' of a deeply religious experience - We search for 'meaning', struggle to obtain 'meaning', can be uncertain or very clear about the 'meaning' of a word, a sentence, a statement, an image, a hand signal, a raised eyebrow, a one finger gesture, an angry look, a work of art, etc. etc.

Meaning is a conceptual entity the form of which can be 'given' to a subject in an experience. We can note phrases such as 'Her work **gives** meaning to her life' 'His religious belief **gives** meaning to his life'. In the mode of self-consciousness, individuals can be liable to psychosis when their lives become 'meaning-less.' The substance of meaning is a necessary, if not a sufficient, condition for human well-being. Sufficiency is realised if that which has meaning can be at least adequately integrated into a functioning life. In communication something **has** meaning, in existential terms something is **imbued with** meaning. But, even as a conceptual entity which is 'given meaning', meaning is not in itself a substance or even a sematic attribute in itself (if it does facilitate semantic sense within our experience), and yet it is perhaps the most essential aspect of our mental lives; it is a conceptual entity that is involved in the representation, transmission, and expression, of information. For Merleau-Ponty (op cit. 1962, p.xix) 'Because we are in the world, we are *condemned to meaning*,....'

Meaning is a purely psychological entity in the sense that its realization is in us rather than in the world from which we encounter and interpret its presence. This as invoked by perception, and developed by conception, within an interactive relationship between self and phenomena. Phenomena as only the slightest of stimuli can involve meaning, even a taste or a smell, can invoke a range of meaning-rich associations. More dramatic phenomena, such as a blast on a car horn or a cry for help, show the potential dynamic immediacy of meaning. While more complex stimuli such as when considering the function of the cerebral cortex or reflecting on aspects of the civil war in Afghanistan (summer 2021), open up veritable waves of meaning-rich associations and implications. These types of meaning-rich evocations tend to be experienced within awareness-based relationships to the external world, but similar evocations are also a fundamental aspect of introspective experience. As activities, awareness and meaning, if inextricably connected, are not the same; awareness is the necessary background for experience, meaning provides semantic significance for the process of awareness.

Bertrand Russell ('The Analysis of Mind', 1921, p190) commenting on the origin of words noted: 'The association of words to their meanings must have grown up by some natural process, though at present the nature of the process is unknown.'

It is this elusive 'naturalness' that points towards our organicity as being the bio-genealogical root of meaning; in evolutionary terms, as a core aspect of our adaptive capacity. As a qualitative mode of any organism's process of making sense of its world. In some ways it is inappropriate to compare meaning in humans and to then apply this to all organisms – but the essential aspects of that which underlies the concept i.e.

73

behaviour-based interpretation and adaptation, applies to any organism's experience. Meaning facilitates adaptation, on the simplest of levels: an amoeba adjusting behaviour according to its bio-level interpretation of the information being processed uses some primitive sense of meaning to interpret, and so adapt to, its 'world' (its re-ality).

Meanings are not themselves representations as such. Although we can use representational language to explain what this or that means to us – and cultures and even groups within cultures have developed 'meaning-rich' interpretive contexts. For all aspects of personal or shared experiences, meanings are better understood as that aspect of thought that allows the semantic granularity necessary for the range of thinking progressing from immediate awareness to clear understanding; so providing the operative element necessary for thinking.

As to what meaning is beyond this more elliptical suggestion - the mean-ing of meaning - it is difficult to say. Meaning is spoken of as being: perceived, felt, seen, intuited, realized, and in similar intentionally directed ways. The process of information acquiring meaning is a personal (subjective) experience but we also speak of meaning being comprehended, so acknowledging that it is also a communicable, outwardly directed, element of experience subject to conventional symbol-systems, especially as in language, moving and still images, and music. There does seem to be an aura of shared possible meanings for any idea, proposition, word, etc. (indeed any signifier) and this enables interpersonal communication in ways that we can at least feel 'satisfied' with – within engagements where meaning is exchanged and realized. We know that meaning is not itself an objective entity (if it can be 'objectified' in semantic terms), it is an ineluctable interpretive medium realised within personal and inter-personal modes. We are psychologically constituted by and we psychologically constitute meaning, all within intentional contexts.

Be-ing and meaning are inextricable. We are so familiar with the concept of meaning in everyday use, but the multiplicity of potential uses hint at a necessarily deeper 'mean-ing of meaning'. No analysis seeking authentic understanding of the human condition should take meaning for granted and avoid any attempt to outline the deeper, if elusive, dimensions of meaning. We can salvage a core meaning from its dilution in everyday usage – meaning is the psychological mechanism by which we access Reality. The semantic roots of our understanding – we exist within a meaning-rich world and it lives, if selectively, within us.

It is as necessary for us to find meaning within information as it is for us to breathe air.

I suggest that meaning in relation to human cognition represents phenomena that spiral down into our organicity and in a strong sense has roots embedded in bio-systems below consciousness. Nevertheless, to be thorough in our analysis, we must follow the phenomenon of meaning as far into the elusive terrain of pre-conscious life as analytic ability allows. I suggest that the entity which the concept of meaning encompasses is even more significant than concepts such as 'awareness' and 'consciousness' in terms of how humans engage with the world. It is an entity inextricably linked to information-processing – the 'how' of processing our experience (the semiotic perturbations that populate awareness). Without meaning awareness and consciousness would be but insubstantial biological modes lacking any reflective substance.

Meaning is the intrinsic property of a 'relationship' (as a process) between something and something else (the sign – be it word, image, sound, emotion, and similar) that it is referring to (the referent).

Meaning can be immediately realised but can also emerge during a process of referring, so ambiguous (indeed mysterious), but so vital for our accessing Reality. This relationship is not just one of interpretation but also one of interrogation. Meaning allows an individual to engage with experience and so to be aware of a sense of presence in the world.

Meaning is the concept that expresses the interpretive substance of our experience, making awareness possible, but meaning for humans is realized in our psychological mode of self-consciousness. That which is constituted by meanings is crucial to 'What it is like....' to be human and, by extrapolation, if we allow that meaning can be expressed in behaviours related to environmental adaptation, then we can identify threads of meaning in all species; if more just a property of perception in most. With humans this link would be significantly more complex, involving the reflective consciousness of self-hood. Meaning is the unifying property of consciousness, the property that allows us to 'make-sense' of experience.

Meaning is a product of our encounter within experience, but meaning also makes the initial encounter possible. It represents an aspect of be-ing that stands forth as an obvious presence and yet any attempted analysis beyond the fairly obvious slips away from comprehension. I think that there is a possible explanation for this ....it (meaning) represents an aspect of being human that provides our adaptational ability, something rooted in our organicity, so can be seen in effect and affect but not as self-subsistent. We can't be conscious of meaning, only of meanings – the 'mean-ing of meaning' is elusive because it is rooted in the lived rhythm of our bodies (blending into our pre- and unconscious selves); similar to our immune and endocrine systems.

Meaning is probably the portmanteau concept to beat all others – at its most obvious we can see it operating within the conventions of a language in its standard correct forms, but even language has writers and readers, speakers and hearers, and each can bring sources of subjective interpretative variation to it use. Meaning can be compared with the wind, invisible in itself but obvious in its operation as embodied in swaying grasses, the moving branches of trees and people hurrying along, heads bent low and coat collars pulled up.

There is meaning by customs and conventions of languages – allowing the possibility for translation between these – but beneath (infusing) this is a realm of meaning allied to our organicity and so to our subjectivity. If simplistic, perhaps when we note that meaning 'dawns on me' we are reflecting the psychological presence of the pathway towards this terrain of pre-linguistic organicity.

Similar to information more generally (and closely linked to this), meaning is an intrinsic property of the form of information that can be processed by each species – for each species there is a meaning-bandwidth (aligned to the information band-width, see above). Meaning is a property of the form of information

76

that can be processed by each species – an implication of this meaning-based processing difference being a species marker. Accepting that within species – most obviously the primates - this range of processing can be subject to individual variation within a wider species-specific range.

I think it would be helpful to view meaning in two ways – firstly, in its conventional (synthetic) form when we gain understanding of an entity by being able to comprehend it in relation to a pre-established symbol system. Symbol systems drawn from our cultural situations, with formal and informal 'rules and conventions' determining semantic interpretation. Where meaning gains a clarity realised in the expression of a word, sentence, text, image. This is the dimension of meaning that is exhibited in systems of communication (primarily languages) – it being rule-bound (both formalised and normative) and liable to take expected forms of expression. Secondly, meaning is an aspect of the information streams that we experience, drawing interpretive forms from deep within our pre-consciousness, even to the extent of our originating organicity. The elusive form of adaptive information processing that is the accrual of our specific species inheritance. These two forms of meaning operate together to invoke the behaviour necessary to engage successfully within a physical or social environment.

So I endeavour to maintain an, albeit artificial, separation between meaning as a key aspect of the social and meaning in its more organic, species-specific, deeper presence – but of course these two modes infuse each other in elusive ways.

Meaning 'emerges' when perceptual and conceptual aspects of experience merge, consciously or pre-consciously, to form some sense, some significant indicator of semantic difference. Sense is an outcome of these aspects being apprehended within a pre-established symbol system. Most obviously a word within a context e.g 'father' within relationships, 'student' within education.

Meaning for human-beings (and in species-specific ways in other animals) is the experiential thread that binds Reality - Language - Thought, together, initially in a subjectivity but which can also relate to collective views of experience (the 'customs and conventions' noted above).

Bertrand Russell ('Analysis of Mind', 1921, Lecture X) considered meaning to be a relationship, and gives the example of the word Napoleon meaning a certain person (if he also acknowledged the relativity of meaning in his later book 'The History of Western Philosophy', 1946). This represents a common view of meaning, as the relationship between a symbol and that which the symbol refers to - the 'sign and the signified'. At a general level this works well for understanding language in use. Words and statements refer to something, even words such as 'is', 'the', 'and', etc. in their connection to other words, in their involvement in sentences and in longer statements, are inextricably involved in this referring. In most ways words are in themselves meaningless in isolation, they have to be placed either in a linguistic or/and a mental (experiential) context. A linguistic context that actually exists, as in a sentence on a page, or a psychological (experiential) context that exists in the imagination. The single word, 'Giraffe' with no other clue to its reference is in itself, as simple presentation, meaningless. It might refer to an animal with a long neck, a code-name for a secret agent, the name given to a computer program, etc. However in our subjectivities (which tend to be uncomfortable with words seemingly lacking meaning) we tend to imagine a context, for most of us we would I suspect (simply because of most common experiential associations) provide the 'long-necked animal roaming about in savannah type country-side sparsely dotted with spiny trees', hence creating a context which then provides meaning for the word Giraffe - any cognitive dissonance is resolved

I suggest that the defining of 'meaning as relation' to reflect but a surface understanding of what meaning involves; valid and pragmatically useful, but superficial. One that appears to work with everyday language but has increasing difficulty as one moves from this to its involvement in describing and explaining more contentious 'sign-situations'.

Meaning is not the relationship between sign and signified, but rather is better understood as the process of moving from (making the connection between) the sign to the signified. Meaning inheres in the psychological 'space' between these.

Let's consider the 'meaning as relation' view even in what appears to be its clearer linguistic form. The meaning of the word Napoleon according to Russell is to be found in the relationship existing between the word and the man referred to, but surely this relationship is merely a convention (David Hume's '... habit of association.'). I suspect some members even of his own army, disaffected (harassed by Cossacks) as they trudge wearily away from defeat at Moscow might have used the words 'That fat little bastard' instead of Napoleon to refer to the same man. Are we to consider that because the ostensive relationship between both Napoleon and the man (Emperor/General), and 'That fat little bastard' and the man, is the same therefore so is the meaning. When in fact the meaning (subsumed within the intentional process of moving from name to description – the interpretive process) of what is being referred to is considerably different in each case; one inextricably generated by intentional perspective. I suggest that if we are to search for a deeper (more creative) understanding of meaning we need to consider that meaning inheres in both the referring symbol and also that which is referred too and that any relationship, possible or actual, that exists between them is simply a type of understanding. That we will need to be considering the 'me-aning of meaning'. To make it clearer for the reader, I have hyphenated the word to stand for the meaning of meaning, which becomes the mean-ing of meaning; the mean-ing of meaning indicates a universal, meanings themselves are related to particulars. It also needs to be understood that mean-ing includes meaning, but the latter is merely the starting point to consider more deeply into (implications of) the former.

Just to clarify where mean-ing fits into the structure of my heuristic analytic, in particular within the 'sign-situation'. The primary relation of mean-ing to sign-situations is that in order to realize meaning in experience, a context has to be formed, the meaning of certain particulars of an experience only emerge in a context. All definitions of meaning seem to agree on this – a contextual framework within some conventional symbol system or within some more personal schema-type sets of ideas. The circumscribing function of sign-situations provides the conceptual context in which meanings can be - intuitively, cognitively, or even imaginatively - most easily realised.

The concept of mean-ing is used to signify the idea of the 'multiplicity' of intentional or otherwise interpretive meanings that are the ever-present possibility of language. Jacques Derrida's concept of 'dissemination' expresses this '...irreducible and generative multiplicity' (see David West, 2012, p205). But mean-ing also signifies the separation of what meaning *does* (the distilled essence of mean-ing in its originating sense) and what meaning *is* in this or that particular context.

So I suggest it would be useful as we now probe further to the inner core of be-ing, or at least (in identifying) conceptual pathways that direct us towards this veiled area of the human condition, to attempt to outline the 'mean-ing of meaning'. That cognitive essence that inheres not in the relationship between two, or more, words (or statements), as between referring 'sign' and any 'signified' referred to. I suggest that mean-ing is the mental activity at the very core of any individual's relation to their experiential world. Mean-ings allow a semantic continuity within interlinked processes of thinking that allow, or at least lead to, awareness and understanding; realized mean-ings are the constitutive elements of each of these psychological modes.

A key analogy is to compare mean-ing to the 'gluon' of high energy physics (the quark-gluon as in the Higgs boson) that gives/allows baryonic mass to subatomic particles. Mean-ing gives/allows 'semantic mass' to thinking. I suggest that this is a particularly relevant analogy and one that indicates an aspect of mean-ing offering potentially informative clues for further consideration by philosophers and psychologists.

For humans, mean-ings themselves are rarely clear-cut thoughts with single focal points, seemingly specific meanings blend into each other (remember this is within any sign-situation), often only in our pre-conscious mode of thought. Sign-situations, with their intentional substrate, are 'somethings' which arise as we operate within our world. They provide the inherently meaning-infused information into which each organism then realizes specific meanings, and from which it subsequently draws understanding. I mentioned organism in the last sentence in order to draw attention to the implications of mean-ing when placed in an evolutionary context. In human beings the development of the search for mean-ing generally results in understanding. If only confusion results then mean-ings have been misunderstood in relation to the meaning-being's life; the confusion of meanings remain only a mixture of feelings and emotions, the meanings have not developed. Probably owing to the lack of any articulate 'context-connection' being realized; or on a simpler level, even of any more immediate associations being made.

When we consider that we understand something this usually means that a linguistic formulation in its broadest terms has been established, or at the very least a person who is not involved in purposely deceiving another or themselves can say they understand something at least sufficiently in relation to any purpose. Searching for, absorbing, and generating, meaning is our primary communicative relationship to the world. Organisms, from the simplest to the most advanced (in information-processing evolutionary terms), have in common the ability to process information that arises as they move within their habitats. By processing this information they can maintain homeostasis, seek out and ingest nutriments, avoid potentially harmful encounters, etc. An aspect of this survival behaviour being that organisms are able therefore to adapt (within their species limitations) in order to survive.

For all organisms mean-ing is gained when 'thought', or whatever is the equivalent processing modality for any organism, finds its 'repose'. The subjective hunger for making sense ('integrative' as in Gestalt psychology) of a world is, if only temporarily, satisfied. If any organism possess sufficient information-processing ability it can progress beyond isolated primitive meanings to higher levels of cognition as we move into a world composed of knowledge and understanding. I hope the consideration of meaning from an organic (evolutionary) perspective allows some understanding of the primitive, indeed primary, implications of mean-ing.

Human-beings differ from other organisms mainly in terms of the complexity of the information we can process (both quantitatively and qualitatively) and the fact that we have a different relation to the information being processed, we can 'hold' related information within our minds; if within the general fluxion of thought processes. This is because we are self-conscious beings, and the related patterns of information that we can hold or re-present in awareness form the conditions for the understanding that has developed during our initial mean-ing-infused encounter within our world. This assimilated information can then form the material for memories, planning, imagination, and other forms of cognitive processing.

A simple analogy that might help to reveal the relationship between mean-ing and understanding would be that the perception/conception of meaning with-in the discontinuous flow of information can be compared to a series of lights coming on in the brain and the combined illumination cast by clusters of pre-conscious lights provides the cognitive 'illumination' leading to (underlies) the understanding, so allowing us to operate with-in the world; and, as with illumination, the clarity of understanding can vary in intensity. Compare this with what we know of brain physiology. Neurons are continuously electro-chemically active, but when involved in conscious thought they are activated beyond a threshold level, 'illumination spreads'. Enabling a sense of awareness that provides the psychological conditions for specific meanings to emerge. Localized groups of neurons, interconnected to wider brain regions, link together to form intricate patterns of activated neural networks related to any experience, or in my terminology, a sign-situation.

This is of course an ever-moving process as neurons 'enter' or 'leave' any sign-situation related thought process; with activated neural patterns flowing around the brain and any other parts of the nervous system involved. I am groping for a way of expressing this multi-layered, elusively complex, process, able to change with the speed of electro-chemical action, each circumscribed experience (as single signs or developing sign-situations) involving potentially millions of neurons in ever-changing wave-like patterns. We have a serious problem of being unable to find any analogies or metaphors that are convincingly adequate to express even just the physiological operation of the brain – the brain is beyond the current meaning-horizons of our language; we lack the descriptive, let alone the explanatory, capability. Thinking at an individual level operates according to a multi-factor dynamic involving, intentionality, the unpredictable memory system, feelings, emotions, biological drives (hunger, thirst, sexuality, fear, uncertainties), and much more.

A critic might now accuse me of common materialism with my appearing to reduce mean-ing and understanding to a physiological level of description. I used the two analogies:

1. That between lights and illumination as analogous to meaning and understanding.
2. That between related neuron-sets and wider neural-networks as analogous to (correlated with) mean-ing and understanding.

Noting neurons and the other bio-electro-chemical material making up the physiology of the human nervous system is simply the description at a certain type of material level explanation. I could perhaps, given sufficient knowledge, have described the brain in sub-atomic, 'energy' (quantum) terms. Or have given a highly abstract description of mental activity, as might reflect a philosophically convincing outline, with which to express consciousness.[10] But we currently lack an explanatory mode that can even just sublate the material brain and the non-material mind within some higher-level description of the operation of human information processing.

Mean-ing, understanding and their relationship would not be adequately described as bio-electro-chemical activity taking

---

[10] I think that the criticism by those such as Patricia and Paul Churchland of our application of a crude 'folk language' (arising from a 'folk psychology') to describe/explain aspects of consciousness is valid. We do retain and apply a pre-used language, with perhaps the addition of some more modern (often information technology based) metaphors/analogies, to new information. But I have doubts about their suggestion that advancing neuroscience will generate a dramatically improved terminology designed to overcome such issues as the 'brain/mind' disjunction. Even if it might be able to incrementally improve description and explanation in terms of a terminology it will be inadequate if phrased in any form of reductionist, material, ways – seeking some sophisticated neuro-scientific 'language' designed to describe/explain thinking in terms of physiological brain-states.

place within the nervous system.[11] Although for certain limited purposes this has been shown to be a useful level of description, one that has assisted advances in cognitive psychology, in particular in the area of psychological pathology. More advanced consideration of brain physiology, as in a consideration of the implications of the evidence of what might underlie 'neural correlates of consciousness', are informing the progress of neuro-psychology and neuro-philosophy, if as yet these have been inadequate to explain thinking as an experienced phenomenon in material terms.

We do have a sense that mean-ing and understanding arise in an awareness physically and psychologically located within the brain; their seemingly being manifested as relationships between patterns of activated neurons. But this only conveys a partial picture of mental activity and ignores the underlying involvement of all the active, but not consciously activated aspects of nature, nurture, memories, and similar subjective material. It also ignores the external stimulus and the effects of the experience of being a 'body' moving, imaginatively and actually, around in the world.

To clarify: Neuronal activity, however accurately it comes to be described, is not 'thought' - not unconscious, preconscious, or conscious. It would be misleading to link these by anything other than a very suggestive form of correlation based on intertwined necessary conditions. In due course neuroscientists will no doubt apply a usefully reductive type of investigative analysis to the central and peripheral neural systems and so be able to outline a detailed description of their functional arrangements. But such descriptions will be inadequate (indeed inappropriate) to explain thinking; the constitution of thinking elusively transcends bio-electro-chemical activity. If such activity is itself a necessary condition for the interlinked processes in which inheres the affective dispositions. We require a new form of language developed by an evolved understanding, one that can

---

[11] If we want to better understand the relationship between neural activity and sign-situations it would be necessary to seek some more satisfactory description of what we mean by 'material', but this is not the place to do more than flag-up this implication.

more adequately express the mediating relationship between these layers of human mental life. From the organic perspective, the understanding sought, via mean-ing, as an organism reacts within its environment, is sought in order to enable it to adapt to changing environmental stimulus and its own changing intentions in relation to its world (its own lived re-ality). I would go so far as to suggest that the human craving for meaning is even more fundamental than the bio-psychological cravings for hunger, sex, and thirst; we are predisposed to invest 'meaning' in what we experience, we, are uncomfortable without it.

As Koestler ('The Ghost in the Machine', 1967, p82) noted: 'The meaning we attach to this sound-pattern [of words] is agreed by conventions of language. But man has an irrepressible tendency to read meaning into the buzzing confusion of sights and sounds impinging on his senses; and where no agreed meaning can be found, he will provide it out of his own imagination.'

But, as with the cravings noted above, so also the search for mean-ing is rarely satisfied for long in a conscious human-being, it is the dynamic core of our (indeed all 'information-processing' organisms) be-ing-in-the-world.

I have endeavoured to show that the idea that mean-ing is to be found in a connection between a symbol (or even a sensation) and something referred to, is only a beginning to analysing the full involvement of mean-ing within the human condition. If I cannot be clearer than I have been, that I have not held the 'mean-ing of meaning' up to be considered from all potentially relevant perspectives, then I think that this is a reflection of its elusive bio-psychological constitution.

With a more developed mental activity, such as in understanding, this is usually present in forms that can be tested, the type of understanding might be variable, (person to person exposed to the same set of 'mean-ingful-stimuli', or even the same person at different times), but it can be quite clearly outlined. A simple example being that: you can expose a person to the word 'Napoleon', then point to a picture of the once formidable French General, you enquire; does the person now understand what this word refers to. If the subject then says he understands the word to relate to a picture of a short, tubby, man in white pants his 'mean-ing net' has probably not captured the sense you were trying to convey, and you will need to provide the additional information, more specifically relevant to your intention regarding the form of understanding you wish to invoke in the subject. Perhaps highlighting the general's relatively humble beginnings, the extent of his subsequent military achievements and the European empire he created. Misunderstanding is an indicator of the polysemous implications of meanings, including their 'sticky fluidity', but also implying an inherent potential for correction or clarification.

So, to sum up where we are: I started by considering, in relative detachment, Reality - Language - and Thought, each of which having a preliminary defining characteristic. Reality, as complex, Language as synthetic, and Thought as intentional. I then reunited them in their experiential inter-dependence as they infuse within each other to constitute our experience; within Being, our personal 'be-ing' that binds experience. The basic unit of conscious experience being the 'sign-situation' (and constituting signs), with its interpretively fluid content arising primarily from the variable forms of intentionality that the thinking subject brings to any experiential situation. Intentionality can be understood as the subject's contribution to the initial constitution and subsequent development of any 'sign-situation'. 'Sign-situations' provide the experiential context within which perceived meanings are assimilated; these interpreted meanings are then available for the conception of understanding. Note that in the last sentence I wrote of meanings as being perceived and understanding as being conceived but of course meaning does operate throughout, if in different ways. I do this to highlight the balance between the different proportions of bottom-up (perceptual) and top-down (conceptual) sources of the information available; a shifting balance depending on the context of any experience. Each experience represents an infusion of two different types of information processing. In mean-ing the emphasis is on perception, and in understanding the emphasis is on conception. If neither is wholly one or wholly the other.

Mean-ings maintain the pre-conscious link to our organicity, as such they are difficult to clearly define. Language can be about the unconscious (a pre-linguistic or proto-linguistic realm) but it does not dwell within it, this is a realm more of what we might term emotions and feelings, and so one 'side' of a porous interface between these and cognition, memories, calculations, the self-monitoring conscience, and thinking more generally. But access to them is to follow meaning from being a relationship between sign and signified (referring to referent) as a process, into a deeper consideration of the signs and signifiers themselves, this is where the 'mean-ing of meaning' resides, within an elusive but affective, pre-conscious organicity.

So, for me the link between sign/symbol and referent is not a simple form of relation but that it is in the 'process of referring' that meaning emerges - with the form taken by any referent being a variable outcome of this process. The process of referring being very much an individual act involving a person's past experience and more immediate intentionality. A process that yes connects to simples – sign/symbol to referent - but immediately invokes a range of meaning-imbued implications.

In broad terms meaning infuses any organism's adaptation to the world and for humans it enables semantic substance to be experienced. Understanding makes sense of the multi-layered, meaning-infused, fragment of Reality (the re-ality) we each access. Meaning is the interpretive and interrogative interface between the individual (or group) and experience; it allows information to be realized in forms accessible to consciousness.

Chapter 3: Conflictual conditions

The next step is to outline the form taken by the conceptual elements I have brought together to constitute Being as shared by humanity in general and be-ing as a process of selective unification that is a primary feature of individual human cognition.

When we consider any situation, whether simple or highly complex sign-situations (complexity being a function of the informational content), individuals asked to describe what they experience would often give varying answers. Two British middle-aged males describing a white duck would, given the two factors of their being similar types of people considering a quite simple 'sign-situation', very likely offer fairly similar descriptions. But with a economically comfortable middle-aged male and an economically disadvantaged teenager describing what is happening when a police car is passing by, it is more likely that the older man would talk in favourable terms of defending property and keeping the peace, whereas the youth is more likely to be antagonistic and talk in terms of provocation and oppression. Now taking a potentially highly complex 'sign-situation'; A Serb Christian and a Bosnian Muslim each asked to explain what led to the conflict involving the ethnic-based parties to the Federation established following the break-up of the country formerly known as Yugoslavia.[12] We would see entirely different perspectives given the interpretive milieu each group had been immersed in. Whereas the information content of the break-up is 'out there' as factual information, what has been drawn from this accumulation has been limited by intentionally informed interpretive frameworks – we might term the outcome being the social construction of 'different perspectives'. Perspectives that, as in most similar conflictual situations, have

---

[12] The long and detailed history of the antagonistic groups, even preceding the post-WWII formation of Yugoslavia and following its break-up in the 1990s, was characterised by massacres, concentration camps, bombing and shelling and of civilians and hundreds of thousands of refugees forcibly driven out of their homes, or just fleeing conflict.

foundations which lie within inherited narratives and immediate antagonisms, together contributing to form the intentionality underlying today's to-be-applied perspectives.

As the potential for complexity inherent in any antagonistic issue (as a 'sign-situation') increases so potentially more diverse would become the interpretations. To the point when an observer would be inclined to think that such is the divergence in explanations that it seems as if the respondents had experienced entirely different situations. In fact in a novel but relevant (to any disagreement) sense they had! The information contributing to form their perspectives differed markedly. And it is this potential variance in individual and group interpretation, in relation to what a 'neutral' observer might judge to be the same situation, which gives a clue to where I am going.

Individuals are nurtured and socialized in relation to their own reaction to these formative factors, acting as a background influence on the ways in which the mass of information they are exposed to in the lead up to any conflictual situation can be interpreted; a complex set of interactive processes contributing to a psychological constitution would have taken place. The concept of intentionality is used above to encompass the affects of this construction arising out of our experience within be-ing. The terms 'intentional arc' and 'intentional trove' were employed as short-hand for key aspects of the personal background of individual intentionality. The outcome of the involvement of elements of the 'intentional arc/trove' give rise to an individual taking a perspective on any situation; a perspective being the actual form that arises from all the possible formative intentional material lying within an individual's 'intentional arc/trove'. An individual possess only one such intentional resource. Although access to it is only ever partial, and the potentially available meanings ready to become understanding in consciousness, those involved in memories, motivations, prejudices, conscience, emotions, etc, reside mostly in the un, and pre, conscious. Potentially accessible, if not in an easily predictable way. But when this intentional background is exposed to any sign-situation only a single perspective generally emerges; if with the potential to adapt. The 'intentional arc/trove' is fairly wide and ever-present, the perspective taken to any situation is a selection of an individual's wider intentionality involving a usually quite narrow perspective. So, the perspective at the point of any judgement, and/or action taken, involves the considerable narrowing of any individual's intentionality. The intentionality of an individual's partial view (perspective) taken of any sign-situation includes recognizing some 'facts' and 'relationships' as being more significant than others.

It might be suggested that I am simply stating that which is fairly obvious, that individuals and groups, having had different formative experiences will tend to view the same situation in different ways. This is the basic condition of those involved in conflict situations, but it is the formative background as realized in the perspectives of those involved that needs to be rigorously clarified in order to identify possible elements of shared intentional substrate beyond the immediacy of any conflict. Resolution requires seeking some identification of the more determinate elements constituting any perspective, and ideally to highlight any shared concerns. One of these perspectives might be that each side is fearful of the other and that addressing the basis of the mutual fear might begin to allow some alleviation of an issue. I accept that this is a more obvious source of at least some element of potential resolution if, that is, the fear is simply an outcome of unfounded generational suspicions of each 'sides' motives.

Historically most conflict situations have been based on quite naked motives of seeking land, water, slaves, oil, gold, timber, and other valued resources - and 'glory'. So, motives that seem unlikely to be easily amenable to resolution. But the rigorous analysis referred to above might just reveal that even these nakedly obvious aggressive acts, taking seemingly intractable forms, might potentially be usefully re-considered by those involved. Perhaps by enlarging the formative intentional context and with consideration of the probable outcomes of any conflict (including introducing thinking of long-term implications) - see below for a further consideration of this.

When you consider all the disagreements which can cause conflict between individuals, groups, nations, etc. the 'dis-unifying' thread that runs through them is the differences in perspective taken by those involved. Too often actual conflict erupts from but a simplistic assessment of motives imputed by one side of the other. I suggest that understanding the formative circumstances which lies behind the seemingly obvious fact of different perspectives is of critical importance if we are to resolve conflict (reduce the potential for the expression of evil), in whatever personal, social, or international, area it occurs. A corollary of this, in relation to the primary motive for undertaking this entire analysis, is that differential perspective-taking is one of the most significant causes of 'evil' in the World; one that infuses all the others. And differential perspective-taking and all that it implies is of high complexity – if an outcome of potentially de-constructible processes.

It might be argued that inter-personal/group/national conflicts arise owing to a clash of self-interests, represented in perspectives being formed, which are often irreconcilable. But self-interest (as conceived by potential antagonists) is just another judgement made within invariably limited perspectives and if further information were to be made available to antagonists then any conception of self-interest might change. Suggesting a potential terrain on which to find some transcendental grounds for resolution of any local conflict.

If antagonists refuse to accept an alternative interpretation of current, or ignore new, information, and their conception of what is in their self-interest remains impervious to any new information and different considerations, it is possible that they become irredeemably entrenched. Sadly, a condition that seems to pertain in most conflictual 'hotspots' across the world today. In this event, depending on circumstances - interpersonal, inter-group, or between-nation - conflict could potentially be resolved by endeavours to persuade antagonists to reconsider the context of their 'self-interest' (to consider this beyond the immediate issue, from perhaps a longer-term perspective), or by recourse to the interpretative decision-making' of some authoritative body/code that has been accepted as credible by each 'side'.

Coming back to reconsider another aspect of differential perspective-taking in the form that it arises for the individual, I'll begin with a simple example. I see a car speeding towards me, I take the perspective (exercise a judgement) that it is either a stupid motorist, or a stolen car, but when I see flashing blue lights come on and hear a siren, I switch to a 'police-car after law-breakers' perspective. All three perspectives (not necessarily as definite as making judgements) have behind them a considerably narrowed section of my 'intentional arc/trove', and the enormous amount of potentially accessible knowledge stored within it. As new information becomes available, and the initial sign-situation is radiating away from its initiating core centred on the speeding car, I modify, or even significantly alter, the perspective I am taking. Given this, I would suggest it to be useful, if a clearer understanding of Being and its subjective (personal) dimension 'be-ing' is what we seek, if we consider all perspectives taken, and any judgements made as a result of them, to be but provisional.

This acknowledges the fact that any judgements-descriptions-explanations are made within perspectives that are invariable limited; if sufficient for most circumstances. Limited either by a lack of knowledge (information) related to any situation, or by the disingenuous position adopted by those involved. The fact that to be diligent we need to assume that provisional is a necessary prefix to any judgement-description-explanation does not detract from the value these might have to living our life, it is merely (but 'merely' in an important sense) drawing attention to their epistemological status – determined by necessary cognitive and other limitations. This provisionalism, the recognition that we might not have sufficient information to make judgements in our own or our group's longer-term interest, reveals a starting point to begin a consideration of any disagreement, and also perhaps a possible reflective route to conflict resolution.

With all human behaviour, there is a connection to our evolutionary heritage, here with our tendency to make an early assessment of situations (sign-situations) before taking into account all the possibly available information. It could be another residue of an organism's need to react quickly if they are to adapt successfully to changes in their local environment. Best not to wait too long while you analyse movements in nearby bushes, but to make the narrow evaluation that the movement is sufficiently similar to that made by a sabre-toothed tiger therefore calls for a hasty, if quiet, retreat from the area. This is a very simple example of the fact that our perspective tends to be narrowed to what we consider to be of importance to our more immediate lives and that judgements have to be made in order to operate successfully in our world. Whether that would be a relatively primitive one of early humankind, with all its immediate dangers, or the world of civilized peoples operating perspectives and making judgements usually related to only narrow (enculturalized) conceptions of self-interest as discussed above. I focus on the individual but I suggest that this can be projected onto the group perspective, not least due to the approach taken between groups in relation to any conflictual issue being primarily an outcome of the perspectives taken by leading agents within these

I consider the conception of differential perspective-taking to be useful to the understanding and so the potential resolution of conflict at whatever level, personal, group, nation, etc. The therapeutic use of Cognitive Behaviour Therapy (CBT) in psychotherapy being an implicit recognition of the importance of perspective and of its potential flexibility if new, or a reinterpretation of current, information, is available. This basic approach has been shown to be especially useful in fostering the resolution of personal 'mental' (psychological conflict) suffering. Given the verging on psychotic political condition of much of the world some resetting of national and global political perspectives seems to be a necessary condition for the well-being, if not the actual survival, of humankind.

Daniel Kahneman (2011- Nobel Prize winning economist and Senior Scholar at Princeton University) posited two systems of thinking processes that, if somewhat crude generalizations do offer an interesting and informative perspective on human cognition. One (System 1) operating quickly, being based more on unreflective insight, representing our immediate reaction to any experience. The other (System 2) being a form of cognition operating more slowly, to monitor and adjust System 1 thinking in line with wider considerations. But such is the ever-evolving nature of thinking processes that the two systems are always involved in awareness (awareness is a process of continuous change – again W.James's 'stream of consciousness'). For

Kahneman: '.....System 1 generates surprisingly complex patterns of ideas, but only the slower System 2 can construct thoughts in an orderly series of steps.' System 1 being more about our immediate reaction to experiences (intuitions, feelings, impulses, impressions, as well as prejudices and socialized assumptions) whereas System 2 is more about self-directed processes such as accessing memory, conscience, examining and proposing arguments, and monitoring oneself in social situations. System 1 processes are automatic, immediate, and require little mental effort. System 2 operates more slowly as it more consciously allocates attention to aspects of an issue that have been identified as important. Both systems operate when we are awake and there are no physically discrete areas of the brain allocated solely to one system or the other. The interaction of the two systems is what Kahneman terms '....a psychodrama with two characters.'

The immediate-reflective aspects of judging and thinking more generally, although admittedly crude conceptualizations of thought (Kahneman himself, calling them 'convenient fictions' – so heuristic) had been noted much earlier by the philosopher David Hume in the eighteenth century, summed up in his comment: 'In every judgment which we can form concerning probability, as well as concerning knowledge, we ought always to correct the first judgement, derived from the nature of the object, by another judgment, derived from the nature of the understanding.' (Hume, 'A Treatise of Human Nature', 1738 - p177 vol.1 of Everyman ed. 1911)

Whether Kahneman's 'System 1' or Hume's 'first judgment' being modes of thinking informed by only limited information – leading to more dispositional than considered judgements. This immediate thinking is more likely to be characterized by stereotyping, prejudice, noting differences rather than similarities, and similar more superficial characteristics of the 'other', or when interpreting events. Seeking to accommodate to dispositional expectations involving preformed schemas and ingrained selective categories. Then, as thinking progresses beyond the immediate, the unique aspects of a sign-situation (i.e. as more information is internally and/or externally generated) can be considered, possibly leading to adjustments to initial considerations. So accommodating perspectives more towards the actual situation rather than interpreting actual situations to suit limited preconceptions.

It is of course possible that more reflective processes of thinking will merely confirm initial judgements, ones now reinforced by additional selectively interpreted information. But it might also be that widening the informational context can adjust thinking in more positive ways. Bear in mind that I am focusing on potentially antagonistic sign-situations.

I suggest that there are four primary constituting elements influencing perspective-taking:

Socialization – This encompasses the influence of our upbringing and the social context within which our lives are circumscribed (our encluturalization) – sources of powerful, verging on the determinate, influences on how we engage with our lived experience. In both interpreting our experience and how we represent this to others.

Within the wider context provided by socialization there are the elements of 'assumptions' and 'intentions', both of which can be conscious or unconscious:

Assumptions - This is the source of stereotypes, prejudices, and our inherent tendency to project what are for us 'givens' as we assess (make judgments about) any individual's behaviour, or any social or political issue.

Intentions – This involves purposes usually related to a conception of self-interest. The more immediate aims of an individual or collective body (e.g. 'national interest') set within a wider intentional background. With the elements of immediate and background intentionality infusing and informing each other in response to more situational factors.

Situational factors – These involve the influence of the immediate social context an individual is placed or in any setting operating to produce a group perspective. The powerful influence of group-mentality can been seen in the fictional 'Lord of the flies' novel, and at an extreme in collective suicides (The Jonestown, Heaven's Gate, Solar Temple, and Doom's Day mass religious suicides), or murderous tribal-based action Nigeria (1960s) and Rwanda (1990s), and the jingoistic national and ethnic mass hysteria seen across the globe throughout the 20th century. These last most tragically in the wasting of millions of military and civilian deaths, the destruction of infrastructure, the widespread pollution of land and seas, and the squandering of vast amounts of money in the two world-wide wars.

More prosaically, but offering persuasive evidence, the social scientist Philip Zimbardo (following up on the dramatic conclusion of his infamous 'prison experiment') brought together in his book 'The Luther Effect' (2007) a range of experimental findings, and more natural situations, to show the power that groups (expectations) can have on individuals, and more generally the impact that various elements of a 'situation' can have on behaviour. And of course, throughout civil history, there has been the willingness of individuals to concede their moral autonomy and to 'follow orders', whether this be individuals involved in the Nazi action to exterminate, trades unionists, communists, Jews, the disabled, homosexuals, gypsies and others, during WWII, those who have knowingly dropped bombs or fired missiles into civilian residential areas, and those down to today ordered to take action leading to suffering of non-combatants in numerous conflicts. In summary: the intricate but powerful psychological influences that arise in stimulating a tribe, ethnic-group, nation, gang, etc. to behave in ways that go beyond what the composing individuals might consider acceptable when on their own.

All of the references to: 'more likely', 'tendencies', 'possibilities', 'probabilities', 'sometimes', etc. that are used above, are not I hope due to my seeking to protect my analysis against possible criticisms and instead they more simply reflect the extent of our ignorance about the motivational factors influencing outcomes – an acknowledgment that human behaviour is not determined – but is in fact about 'more likely', 'tendencies', 'possibilities', 'probabilities', 'mores', 'sometimes'.

Most sexually abused children do not go on to become

96

abusers, some 'saints' do, some individuals stand against the group, some pacifists reject the warlike jingoism of a nation, some children reject the political or religious extremism of parents, some soldiers have refused to obey orders to fire on women and children – so defying common more deterministic assumptions. More generally, most of us endeavour to do good rather than harm; if our conscience reminds us of situations where we might have done more of the former and less of the latter. In behavioural terms, we humans can seem like emotional enigmas wrapped in sensuous bodies.

From a wider perspective we can seek to create economic conditions, construct institutions of national and international law, and design political arrangements, that we know promote the good and minimise the potential for harms.

Numerous situations where individual autonomy can be witnessed provide persuasive evidence that humankind can collectively change the direction taken by civil life – can bring more humanistic values to bear on our future. We, as individuals and collectively, are not necessarily condemned to drag the accrued dysfunctional economic, social, and political institutions to which evil clings, with us into the future.

This is the social terrain within which normative narratives are formed, most obviously within nationalisms, ethnicities, tribalisms, and religions. And here the perception of any group's self-interest is conceived and projected primarily by controlling elites.

As noted earlier, this outline investigation of the human condition, especially in relation to thinking, had the theme of 'why evil' and I want to consider the causative factors for this in the context of institutional systems (economic), nation-statehood (nationalism), and group (ethnicity).

We have the propensity to hold different perspectives on major issues such as currently: the Israel/Palestine impasse, a number of conflicts (ethnic-based antagonisms) between the nations of former Yugoslavia, the civil wars in Syria, Libya, Yemen, and Somalia, 47m people in poverty in the OECD countries (rich nations), 8% of the world's people living in 'extreme poverty', 13m child refugees with 17m more if still in their own countries also displaced due to conflict, the treatment of Uighurs in western China, the treatment of Rohingya in Myanmar, the treatment of migrants across much of the world.... to note but some current issues through which the tendrils of evil starkly trail.

In relation to perspective, for each of the three areas noted - institutions, nations, groups - the perspective is primarily formed within an influential aura of dominant ideologies advanced by controlling elites in nations and leaders within various types of group, with civil institutions (religious-governance-media-education etc.) designed to serve these. The perspectives taken on any issue invariably reflect the interests of each entity as perceived by those in control – those who inherit the maintenance and regulation of any dominant ideology or religion.

If different, and narrow (so partial), perspectives are taken by those involved in any conflictual situation, then how can the conflict be resolved? I suggest three possible ways:

- By the use threat or use of violence, with the most militarily powerful being the likely 'winners'.

- By negotiation – a seemingly useful approach but one again most obviously prone to the most powerful party (economically, militarily, or power of those already occupying disputed territory) taking advantage of asymmetric conditions of power.

History shows that both of these commonly adopted options can mostly only settle disputes on a temporary basis. With the losers in conflict or the weaker party disappointed with outcomes of negotiations each nursing grievances, each embittered, so providing the source for national or group narratives of injustice down the generations, liable to be expressed in ongoing animosity and future conflicts.

- An untried alternative to the first two being a more transcendent approach, seeking to design processes that produce outcomes that are acknowledged as fair (just) by each 'side' in any conflictual situation. One endeavouring

98

to produce long-term resolution.

This last option is far easier to state than is the task of '.....seeking to design processes....' as noted. A fundamental pre-condition at the international level would be the willingness of nation-states, or for any groups involved in dispute, to concede autonomy (sovereignty for nations) to another form of authority; be this a judicial-type tribunal, a formal code, or mixture of these. There would also need to be confidence in the form of authority that autonomy (sovereignty) is to be ceded too. I think the authority would need to be derived from a pre-agreed constitution, whether this is based on human rights legislation (more appropriate for groups), or on international law as set out in a charter for nations. But of course, there would have to be a level of confidence in those charged with interpreting charters and constitutions that they would be impartial, fair, and focused on the identification of just outcomes.

For inter-nation conflict we already have the aims and principles of the United Nations as set out in its 1946 Charter as subsequently amended (see Appendix I below for some of these aims and principles). Aims and principles that embodied the wisest spirit of human ideals set out following a war that had engulfed most of the world. But the UN as an institution has witnessed the same form of self-seeking international diplomacy based on naked power and mendacious commentaries as had its predecessor, the League of Nations. Both institutions whose aims were vulnerable to the flaws of members (nations) intentions and a lack of the primary necessary pre-condition of a willingness to cede sovereignty in key areas of international relations; not least the right to wage war.

I will return to this global political context following a digression to consider international relations:

The twentieth and early twenty-first centuries have been characterised by destruction – of property, of government finance, of the environment, of lives, and of hopes for humanity's future – in a series of wars interspersed with numerous more localised killing fields as nations – and within nations, ethnically, religiously, or politically, divided groups – clashed on the battlefield and also in the countryside and on the streets of towns and cities. Is there something deep within the nature of humankind that will invariably find expression in violence? Or are we led into conflict due to institutions of governance and the patterns of international relations, and more generally of global political tropes inherited from the past, made even more terrible by the advancing technology of weaponry? Provisionally we might assume that elements of both could be involved, and so our focus would be on mitigating the malign influence of each.....our human nature and our inherited civil institutions.

The Janus-faced countenance of our species – a moral side prone to co-operation and peaceful co-existence and a more aggressive side prone to competition and conflict – was clearly seen in conditions of international relations in the first half of the twentieth-century. The utter futility of WW I with its mud-curdling, blood-curdling, insanity followed by the enlightened setting up of the League of Nations (1920) to arbitrate between nations in dispute. The preamble to its constitution noted that its aims were: 1) To promote international co-operation 2) To secure international peace. Aspirations reinforced with the signing of the Kellogg-Briand Pact in 1928 (more formally: 'The International Treaty for the Renunciation of War as an Instrument of National Policy'). A treaty initially based on an agreement arranged between Aristide Briand (French P.M) and Frank Kellogg (US Sec. of State) that the two states would agree to renounce war. Given more general substance in a bi-lateral agreement signed by: India, Turkey, Germany, UK, France, Spain, Soviet Union, USA, China, Norway, Canada, Australia, Japan.....and about 50 other countries.

The authority of the League was terminally eroded with its attempts to mediate being in effect ignored on a regular basis throughout the 1920s and 30s, and the noble aspirations of the K-B Pact being ignored by the world's most powerful signatory nations as the world was plunged by them into yet another war engulfing much of its population. At this war's end, many European towns and cities were devastated, Japan had been scorched by visitations of hell from the sky, and much of the globe was still being argued over by European nations only being at best grudgingly prepared to accept the post-war surge for

100

independence across much of the colonized territories.

At this second global war's end we again see the moral side expressed in the establishment of the United Nations in 1945.

The purposes of which was noted in its constitution as:

'The purposes of the Organization should be:

1. To maintain international peace and security; and to that end to take effective collective measures for the prevention and removal of threats to the peace and the suppression of acts of aggression or other breaches of the peace, and to bring about by peaceful means adjustment or settlement of international disputes which may lead to a breach of the peace;

2. To develop friendly relations among nations and to take other appropriate measures to strengthen universal peace;

3. To achieve international cooperation in the solution of international economic, social and other humanitarian problems; and

4. To afford a centre for harmonizing the actions of nations in the achievement of these common ends. '

Then followed about 100 more conflicts, including India/Pakistan partition, Korea, Vietnam, Afghanistan, Iraq, Kosovo, Somalia, Nigeria, Israel/Palestine on......actual wars involving the world's more powerful nations or what were, in effect, proxy wars fought with their support. It seems that we have the wish (and the moral intuition) to realise the futility of warfare and the need for international institutions to prevent these, and yet powerful elements of national leaderships have considered an easy recourse to violence as being a legitimate way to conduct international relations; to progress their perception of their nation's interest.

The costs of war in just human terms (omitting the destructive impact on built and natural environments) is significant, with the two World Wars of the 20th century alone taking 95 million lives (50 million of these being civilians – WWI 20m dead with 10m of these being civilian, WWII 75m dead with 40m of these being civilians). Since WWII came to an end there has only been 2 days when there has been not conflict between at least two nations; these being the 2nd and 28th Sept 1945. About 100 more wars since 1945 added about another 10m casualties (again disproportionally civilians) - Korea, Vietnam, Algeria, Russian *invasion of Afghanistan, Chinese invasion of Tibet, American (and allies) invasion of Iraq and Afghanistan, etc. In sum: 200 million plus have died as a result of 20th and early 21st century warfare, over half of these being civilians.*

It is an estimate that in the 5,000 years since the beginning of recorded history, from 3,000 BCE onwards, only about 268 years had no recorded warfare. Just consider the material destruction and human dislocation, death, and general misery caused by this seemingly systemic collective human behaviour. Just consider the economic resources poured and continuing to pour into military preparation and the actual expression of international conflict. Today the global spending on the military is running at $2 Trillion (2020) per year, with the three highest spending nations being Russia $65 Billion (2019), China $261 Billion (2019), and the USA $731 Billion (2019); and these all on rising trends. A waste of resources on a vast scale each and every year – just consider what could be done with such funding for good rather than as preparation for evil in the world.

What sense can there be in young people from different countries, who have themselves never met, coming together with the intention to kill each other. What sense is there in launching missiles, and dropping bombs on cities, towns, and villages, when experience shows that most of the casualties will be non-combatant civilians, including many children? What sense is there in turning civil infrastructures into rubble, farmland into wasteland, and waterways into toxic flows? All being just the more obvious impacts of military conflict.

The consequent question to engaging in such a nonsensical activity would be......... Whose interests are being served by fostering such inter-nation conflict? Who benefits from our living in a world where international diplomacy is pervaded which an overwhelming aura of between-nation antagonisms and background conditions of aggressive economic competition and political hegemony? I would like to, just briefly, consider some of the more obvious aspects of this question.

More recently the most obvious interest would the vast fortunes made by arms companies, various types of 'security' companies, and invariably financial speculators. Then there are political leaders endeavouring to deflect opposition to domestic economic and/or political failure. Or due to the more insidiously mundane fact that for our current national leaders an alternative perspective (based more on the longer-term 'interests' of the whole world's people) does not form an aspect of their mindset. Today's leaders have been politically nurtured to interpret international relations primarily in terms of aggressive economic competition and threatened or actual military conflict. This is their psychological 'comfort zone', one infused by an intentional perspective based on assumptions gained during their socialization within this or that, usually quite privileged (elitist) socio/political context. And these represent just the primary interests served by the conflictual milieu that pervades international relations.

I wish to focus on international relations here, but of course within-nation civil wars have been and are also significant expressions of evil. In places such as Yemen, Mali, Afghanistan, Somali, Myanmar, Tigray, DCR, Libya, and Turkey, communities are currently being torn apart by inter-group violence: groups divided by religion, ethnicity, criminality, tribalism, or by political ambitions. I would expect that if we can outline a viable alternative to global governance than that which currently pertains, this would also contribute to providing conditions, including political mechanisms, conducive to at least easing within-nation conflicts.

If international relations based on sovereign nation-statehood at least pretend (is assumed) to be suitable for overcoming the primary issues facing the world's people then recent history alone suggests that this is a seriously flawed assumption.

And failure in any one of the four critical issues will impact on significant numbers of the global population:

- Environmental degradation.
- Warfare (military conflict), both conventional military engagement and possibility of nuclear catastrophe.
- A.I. and its implications
- Significant and increasing economic inequality (of more importance, significant poverty).

We have inherited an international system that assumes

103

conflict and competition, but can we learn to re-set how we live together? A key element of world governance would be the need to address the role (purpose) of the nation-state.

Nation states in their modern types are a relatively recently established form of political organization (for Jürgen Habermas 1969, p109, 'State and nation have fused into the nation-state only since the revolutions of the late eighteenth century.'), with institutions effectively designed by generations of elite groups (those who, as a class, have accumulated both hard and soft power to themselves). Institutions designed in their own perceived interests, as aided initially by the printing press and national education systems as each contributed to creating and spreading the use of common version of national languages, and assumed national histories. And more recently aided by a xenophobic mass media run/controlled according to corporate interests, often as guided by billionaire owners who assume the privilege to interpret news and produce info- and enter-tainment in line with their own reactionary political views. Mass populations, from earliest childhood until old age, are being drenched with information in forms redolent of the competitive, conflictual, 'mindset' that determines international relations.

Obedience, at times jingoistic enthusiasm, has more often been realised as the default behaviour of the masses, so allowing divisions to be fostered by elite groups able to gain advantage from this depletion (fracturing) of the unifying resources of the masses - a resource with the potential to transcend national borders which were mostly only created on the basis of fiefdoms of local exploitation.

The world's peoples' have been artificially divided ('separated') into nation-states, each with a range of ideas that congeal to create some sense of a 'national interest' which can include the economic (markets and resources), assumed territorial rights, and a self-reflective (too often oversensitive) 'national ego' saturated in selected versions of history; an aspect of the' imagined community 'noted by Benedict Anderson (2006 ed.).

The early civil history of political organization, circa 3,000 BCE, was characterised by city-states as circumscribed units of centralized power; if with some at times expedient regional *federations of these. As certain cities, or federations, became more powerful (in terms of ambitious leaderships and surplus material resources available to equip and support armies) they sought to expand their control, and more widely their hegemonic influence. This developed into empires, some more prominent ones have been: Mesopotamian , Macedonian, Mauryan, Roman, Islamic, Gupta, Han, Inca, Mogul, British, Ottoman, and Hapsburg. Empires each constituted by a multiplicity of ethnic groups, with most being run by an elite section of a dominant one of these.*

Up to about 1500 CE. by far the majority of the world's people, even within empires, had lived their lives within an identity based on the quite local and in accepting the power (control) of some more regional or city-based hierarchy with a variety of types of feudal lord or chieftain at its head. In Europe, it was from this class of lordships and chieftains, along with a wider aristocratic class, that sought to dominate the earliest of states being formed during the almost continuous conflict that characterised medieval Europe. By the end of the sixteenth century much of Europe had been divided into individual 'states' (not nations – states are about centralizing power and control, nations are about these plus various forms of constituting identity) run by elite groups, gaining authority by assumed heredity rights, by the power of arms, and by the disinterested or fear driven obedience of the peoples they sought to exploit.

In addition to the contribution of printing and national education systems to the formation of nation-states noted above, the 15th/16th century voyages of 'discovery' , and associated mapping of the world, provided a territorial perspective serving to provide graphic representation of potential areas of trading or more directly controlling interests (exploitation). The processes of forming the large volunteer or, from about the 1790s conscripted, military units developed to fight European wars, also contributed to forming national mythologies – with impressive statues and other monuments constructed to remind populations of this archly edited past. These, and some other less obvious processes, created the cloying notion of a national identity which could then underline the idea of some 'national interest' and for providing some assumed authority for an aggressive approach to foreign policy.

The European types of nation statehood provided models to be adopted, if more-often only awkwardly adapted to local circumstances, by ruling groups across the world. And, primarily for European elites, nationalism became an artful means of legitimising imperial expansion and exploitative forms of colonialism. It was the European nation states, increasing influenced by powerful merchants, financiers and the senior military, that enthusiastically engaged in shameless international conflict over land, trading rights, and other resources in the Americas, the Middle and Far East and, by the 18ᵗʰ century, Africa.

European nation-states were created during processes of military conflict, economic exploitation, often violent between-nation competition over trading rights and in seeking primary resources. It was these intentional elements that served as core determinants constructing national institutions and shaping the approach taken to foreign policy. The perception of the world as being there for the taking, assuming competition over valued goods in what were assessed as being a zero-sum game, with each nation determined to gain as big a share of the loot as possible. Seeking to advance its elite constructed notions of national self-interest, at whatever cost in sweat, blood, and lives, to indigenous peoples.

It is the 19ᵗʰ and 20ᵗʰ versions of strategic military, economic, and diplomatic, strategies based on systemically operative notions of national self-interest, primarily serving the interests of elite groups, that have set the scene for today's international political arrangements. Arrangements, prominent in which are the more powerful 'empires of influence' (China, USA, and Russia, today) – if underlying these there is the dislocated empire of global finance. All of the world's people are now inveigled within the global conspiracy of assumed division/fracture.

In terms of conflict, actions taken at the international level are more often justified by leaders as being motivated by some conceptual entity termed the 'national interest'? But what constitutes the substance of this concept? Noam Chomsky (2012, p196) noted the 'national interest' as being a form of nation-state international perspective that is something

'....abstracted from [the] distribution of domestic power.' Highlighting how this national interest is created within any country primarily to reflect elite group priorities – those who have domestic power. Be they: corporations, the mass media, the military, landed aristocracy, political groupings, oligarchs, religious leaders, financiers, and speculators. Aided by the armies of lobbyists (and Franz Fanon's other types of modern 'bewilderers') who so determinedly represent them.

International politician–led diplomacy is characterised by a dysfunctional trope compounding suspicion and threatened or actual aggression. Even in a simple form we can understand how symptoms of the consequent disfunctionality can be quite easily identified in various international incidents and in their variable interpretation by nations involved:

In 1983 Soviet planes shot down a Korean Airlines Flight 007, with 269 civilians killed. In 1988 the US guided missile armed cruiser Vincennes, whilst on deployment to the Persian Gulf, shot down scheduled Iranian Airlines Flight 655, with 290 civilians killed. The cause of the Soviet/Korean incident was claimed by the US as 'pure barbarism' and by the Russian as the US using a civilian aircraft to spy on them – neither side would concede that the probable cause was initially a navigational error by the Korean pilot and then a Russian fighter pilot assuming the 'lost' plane to be hostile. The cause of the US/Iranian incident being due to human error in misreading information from the Aegis electronic information system within a military context of regional tension. With the US extraordinarily claiming their action to be a 'justifiable defensive posture'. (I would credit Eric Harth, 1990, p138, with reminding me of these incidents)

The danger of escalation with such incidents is an ever-present possibility - As recently as June 2021 HMS Defender a British warship was on passage through the Black Sea, off Cape Fiolent on the Crimean coast, in what the UK considers to be international waters but Russia views as being within its own territorial waters. A Russian coastguard vessel moved to intercept the warship and a number of Russian S24 jet aircraft flew low over the ship. There were different claims, not just on the legitimacy of the passage, but also on the context of the confrontation. Whoever ordered HMS Defender to take the *route it did (and conveniently took the highly unusual step of inviting a number of journalists to join the voyage) was well aware of the potential for confrontation. Globally, these sorts of hostile/provocative contacts seem to happen on a fairly regular, pretty much 'tit for tat', basis by countries in dispute over some aspect of their assumed sovereignty.*

We might ask why British warships would be 'exercising' in the Black Sea, or why the Russians have increased their own activity in the Arctic Sea. No doubt part of the general provocative activity engaged in by both 'sides'; the military element of hegemonic diplomacy. We might even pose the question.....why 'sides' in a world we share?

And of course – similar types of 'provocation' (brinksmanship) engaged in by other nations: China and Japan over islands in the south-Chinese Sea, India and Pakistan over Kashmir, Ukraine and Russia over the Crimean Peninsula. With most neighbouring unfriendly states undertaking intentionally provocative, sabre-rattling, military manoeuvres in their border regions.

For egoistic nation-states, the narrowing politico/military mindset leads to easily making threats and issuing warning that are difficult to draw back from. The current language deployed in international relations is suited to contributing to quite easily transforming an issue into a crisis and on to escalate into open conflict.

In the 1960s the world was taken to the brink of nuclear war over the Cuban Missile Crisis, an egocentric argument over the siting of Russian missiles on the Caribbean Island of Cuba (the US already had missiles sited in Turkey, close to the Russian border). – We know that some US generals were arguing for a first strike nuclear launch and I think that we can fairly assume that Russian generals have been doing similar urging of their political leadership, and we can be certain that if one side launched then so would have the other - millions killed, extensive infrastructural damage. Simply because the leadership of two nations were engaged in a provocation/reaction political game, the consequences of which could have been far in excess of any rational evaluation of the immediate issue. And interestingly, if a nuclear exchange had taken place then the political leaders and the generals advising them would have been safely ensconced in comfortable underground nuclear shelters whilst all hell broke loose above them; as will those who start any future nuclear conflagration.

Since 1950 there have been 32 documented accidents involving nuclear weapons (and these only the ones known in a context of obsessive secrecy – coded as 'national security') – these 'broken arrow' events highlight the risks involved in the deployment of such weaponry within a fragile political climate redolent of suspicion and fear.

Is there an alternative to international relations based on mutual suspicion and risky military antagonism? The compelling negotiational technique of encouraging antagonists to consider a contentious issue within a wider context, or in relation to a 'higher' idea has been one used on occasion:

In Athens circa 600 BCE a magistrate named Solon was charged with, in effect, writing a constitution for Athens that could resolve the increasingly bitter differences between an elite group of wealthy landowners and most of the rest of the population, including the many small farmers who were continuing to suffer under a debt-bondage system.

Rather than endeavouring to find a system of governance that sought to balance out competing interests in a direct way (probably an impossible task), Solon cleverly tried to raise the 'civil tone' of the ground conditions of governance by seeking what was termed enoumia ('good order'). Setting up a more abstract conceptual 'ideal' by which to justify the constitutional arrangements that he advocated, a concept suggesting that the opposed groups of citizens should consider the longer term interests of Athens rather than only their own short-term class-based advantage. That in the longer-term the ideal of 'good order' would be in the interest of all. A clever 'ideal' deployed to avoid, potentially fruitless, point by point negotiation of differences by positing a higher-level community value that is in the longer-term mutual interest to all parties, transcending their more immediate differences.

Within a few years of his death the political reforms introduced by Solon had been rescinded, due primarily to the resurfacing of

109

old enmities. And in the context of today's even more complex competitive and conflictual world the Solon example might on initial consideration seem to be simplistic, but further reflection could prompt a realisation that the principle element of the example – an appreciation/acknowledgement of a wider (higher) context within which different (even national) competing interests can be subsumed to the overall benefit of all – surely a world at peace, with up to $2 trillion currently spent of armaments available every year for more positive (life enhancing) forms of investment – such as: in pollution control technologies, medical research, education, agricultural improvement, sanitation, etc. - is to be preferred.

In terms of power on a global level, the assumed authority of nation-states to represent the interest of the populations of 193 member-states of the UN is illusory. And this without even considering the extent to which nation-statehood itself actually represents the interests or even the wishes of each nation's population, rather than those of the elite groups who in effect run these countries. Leaving this fundamental question aside, I want instead to focus here on global 'governance'. The concept of global governance (rather than global government) better captures the purpose of designing and introducing a layered system of administration able to operationalise how best the peoples of our world can live together – ideally sharing finite resources in a world with improving environmental and economic conditions, and one avoiding wars and minimising other forms of conflict. The concept of government suggests static representation and assumed power, whereas governance assumes on-going interrogation and a more dynamic approach to co-existence.

Governance suggests design (implying purpose) and invites continuous questioning on any system's value and possible scope for improvement – the best form of governance would be enlightened by a sense of purpose and any related political system would be but a supplementary means of operationalising this. Whereas for nation-state type government purpose is only ever challenged (by internal populations) when significant problems arise. And even then the political classes invariably become more

110

repressive, or in democracies they prevaricate and might reluctantly introduce reforms. This most obviously seen in relation to human rights legislation, or historically in terms of worker's rights and of social provision.

Nation-states have been constructed out of political and social processes and so can in theory be deconstructed and remodelled; or indeed global governance could be re-designed without the divisive presence of nation-states (of a tier of nation-statehood). Perhaps a world without countries would be more of a longer-term ambition than immediately realizable, especially given the nation-based enculturalization experienced by most of the world peoples.

The conflictual tropes generated to advance elite group interests that currently pervade international relations should give way to the language of negotiation, within a wider context that assumes a global interest in peace and co-operation. The mass media and populist politician's terminology – sourced from the xenophobic movie industry, the comic book, the barroom, and the sports-field - and the mendacious language of diplomacy, must be set aside to allow space for the language of negotiation, understanding, and mutual co-operation. And these set within a framework prioritising justice and peace. The forum for the coming together of would-be antagonists must include some judicial/political body tasked with framing issues within a wider global constitution. A constitution not dissimilar to that set out in the UN charter – but unlike that one, a constitution determinedly infusing international relations rather than being some set of abstract ideas retained as a residue of some more enlightened expression of hope, only invoked as but another source of assumed linguistic support to justify short- term national interests. Another layer of deracinated verbiage deployed to veil the hegemonic geopolitics that currently pertains.

If a fair and inclusive system of world governance, based on some tiers of genuine participatory democracy, were ever to be established, it would need to be alert to attempts made by disaffected elite group interests/members seeking to return to nation-statehood by undermining global unifying processes. And the natural inclination of genuine participatory democracy, in relation to communication and the sharing of ideas, will open-up the space for this. The only realistic option (if the curtailing of valued freedoms of expression is to be avoided) is: the efficient management of administration, and open and obviously uncorrupted governance, and continuous vigilance. All in order to continuously prove and promote its value/worth.

But in the anarchic terrain of global communications it does seem that the promotion of obviously dangerous/harmful ideas and obviously false claims ('alternative facts') would require some open media-editing process. Ideally, this would be undertaken by a respected body operating separately from all governments as it interprets pre-establish guidelines arrived at following public debate informed by multiple perspectives (so genuine participatory democracy), tending towards openness and inclusivity, in determining what was acceptable to be shared in any publicly accessible media space. Guidelines to be regularly revisited in order to amend if required in response to ongoing social (including technological) developments.

Is humanity destined to trudge relentlessly and sightless towards its extinction as a species, or can we find an alternative? Any alternative can realistically only be viable if national interests are seen to align to some higher/transcendental aims infusing global economic and political justice and the interests of future generations.

Robust alternatives to nation-driven hegemony can realistically only be based on the recognition of a shared 'international interest' requiring the need to cede sovereignty in areas of primary international concern – be these economic, environmental, or in term of conflict. National interests encompassed within an intentional milieu of mutual respect and genuine co-operation, expressed in a language of unity, cooperation, and collective hope. The intentional element determining global governance should discard elite determined notions of national interest and replace these with governance in the interest of our children and the generations that we hope will follow.....and will do so in peace.

We can note: three necessary conditions for international peace:

- Committing to the terms of the UN Charter (as a Constitution)
- Accepting the authority of those charged to interpret the Charter in relation to particular issues – so agreeing to accept any 'rulings/decisions', perhaps with a right to appeal?
- Ceding sovereignty over key issues, including the right to threaten or wage war

Those elements which differentially contribute to forming any particular (individual, group, tribe, nation) perspective are not 'fixed' they are more tendencies towards interpretations, and as such are socially constructed. Historically influenced as but a part of any current elite-group's interpretive framework. But human beings have the ability, more a constant liability, to reflect. And it is within this reflective capacity where lies the potential to transcend the socialized circumscription of our approach towards understanding our own lives.

Chapter 4: The future confronts us all

Differential perspective-taking and provisionalism are factors which form synthetic limits to the boundaries of thought. Life would be impossibly complicated if they were not primary features of psychological processes. But for the understanding and possible resolution of conflict situations these limiting aspects of thinking (position taking) become of central importance.

Let's see if I can do a bit more with the concept of authenticity on an individual level because without the engagement of committed and determined individuals the institutionalised tendencies towards the expression of evil are more likely to prevail.

Striving for authentic understanding, and to act authentically in ones encounter with-in, existence, means being 'honest' in the best possible sense i.e. existentially rather than legally. Honest as in being true to certain self-formulated ideas, gained during the profoundly personal solitude of self-reflection, to take responsibility for one's own life – an unconditional commitment to seek existential truth. Trying, whenever possible, to go beyond surface understanding and explanations, and also to attempt to separate your own self-interests and potential for bias from your commenting about or understanding any contested 'sign-situation'.

It does not mean that you should be seeking to eradicate personal and intellectual bias, it just means you should endeavour to take them into account, and that this bias (which is a 'natural' propensity) is regularly subject to open scrutiny. Authenticity is intimately related to personal and intellectual integrity. It is about how each of us in our individuality look life with its multi-shifting complexity, dangers, joy and sadness, and the ontic absurdity that the writer Albert Camus so clearly drew attention to, squarely in the 'eye'. Trying to be authentic, and searching for authenticity in our understanding, is the thread of humanity running throughout our task of 'facing absurdity' with all of its uncomfortable existential implications. On the personal level to stand-forth, determined to live rightly in relation to the human values that have been revealed; not least by a number of past and present religious leaders and secular thinkers in both the 'East' and the 'West'. And on the intellectual level to strive for deeper understanding, valuing the power of rational thinking, ever prepared to genuinely reconsider your views in response to the reasoned arguments or suggestive insights of others, or of new information becoming available. Finally, being personally authentic, and searching for intellectual authenticity, is to be prepared to follow the implications of experience to its core (essence) and to accept responsibility for one's own involvement.

Thomas Nagel wrote in relation to the absurd: 'What he [Camus] recommends is defiance or scorn. We can salvage our dignity, he appears to believe, by shaking a fist at the world which is deaf to our pleas, and continuing to live in spite of it. This will not make our lives un-absurd, but it will lend them a certain nobility.'

If perhaps the nobility of a Don Quixote?

For Nagel, Camus's is a 'romantic and slightly self-pitying' view but the insight that allows us to understand the absurd nature of human lives, highlights the limits of the human condition for Nagel, knowing this: '......we can approach our absurd lives with irony instead of heroism or despair.' (Nagel, 1979, pp22-23)

For myself, the process of confronting the absurdity in our lives, reveals the fundamental nature of moral concerns – we come to the conclusion via a comparison in the world of random unjust circumstances for some and equally random unjustified good fortune for others – and of course, to the lack of any reply to our cries of despair about this......the world just continues to enigmatically turn, trailing evil as it does so. We must aim to create a sense of moral nobility by acknowledging the absurd but seeking to transcend this by assuming a life lived in defiance of its seemingly depressing finality, brushing its negative (nay saying) implications aside – it merely serving as a stimulus to our overcoming its pessimistic contaminants. The absurd is not a conclusion. It is but a provisional assessment denying the continuing personal realization (as authentic) of our confronting evil, and also an assessment lacking the consciousness-raising potential inherent within evolving humankind.

As individuals we must be prepared to risk exposure to the full blast of a Reality that constantly buffets the limited certainties to which we cling, as individuals and humankind, like shipwrecked mariners might desperately cling onto drift-wood. The touch-stone of 'human values' - a source of authentic perspective, authentic because these would be values formulated following a reflective consideration of the circumstances of a person's life - as a wider guiding intentional framework from which ones attitude in relation to each particular issue is drawn. The extent to which these align expresses the authenticity of a person's life. Authenticity in itself is a neutral concept in that a person's reflective values could lead to evil ends – some violent political ideology, extremist religious beliefs, or supremacist racial division. Each person commits to their own conscience-driven values as they progress the interrogation of a moral basis for their own lives.

The conditions for authenticity include: clarity of values (and the implications of these for a person's life), personal autonomy, critical self-reflection, consistency, but most of all in assuming responsibility.

As I approach the end of this essay I turn back to a concept introduced at the beginning, that of reason (or rational thinking), a concept synonymous with the best work in philosophy. How best (most effectively in relation to purpose) to apply the organizing framework of reason is probably the most useful thinking process to arise from philosophical speculation. I would argue that it is only of any real use when it is aligned to the realities of everyday life and that the representations generated are accessible to any person motivated to make some effort.

Readers I am sure would have spotted my propensity towards definitions, I consider that these provide a simple starting point to accessing any concept. With reason: Reason could be described as the 'guided seeking for understanding', guided by the intellect in relation to a purpose; there are good or bad purposes but ideally reason initially aims at a neutral evaluation of the facts arising from the consideration of any subject matter (sign-situation).

The concept of reason expresses the ability of humans to interrogate and interpret an issue in particular ways. Involving assessing the veracity of facts and clarifying relationships between these, the justification of any associated claims, examining the logical consistency of arguments, and identifying the implications of judgements and suggested actions. The application of a skill - reasoning - is a neutral activity but it is a process that can be significantly influenced by the purpose of those undertaking any exercise in reasoning. At least in theory, reason has its own determinants of intellectual acceptability that can allow positions/arguments/judgements to be challenged within a mode of credibility. The expectation of intellectual acceptability running throughout reasoning processes, especially in relation to conflictual issues, is the best means humans have to gain an understanding of any issue but also for seemingly competing views to debate these in terms of facts and implications – if these debates must necessarily have to take place within a background context of agreed ethical parameters (some presumption). Even a cursory glance through human civil history and its accumulated results can induce despair – the mostly seemingly rational expression of but narrow self-interests producing an irrational story, and dismal prospects; even if humanitarian values have continued throughout history at least as a presence (so a potential) for the human condition.

A significant issue with promoting the activity of reason is that traditional Western interpretations have overwhelmingly tended to prioritise a form of rationalism that is 'logo-centric'. In philosophy this has allowed description, analysis, and explanation, to assume a certain type of expression that involves the translation of the spoken word into mostly restricted written forms and these with an underlying trope of progression from questions/claims, to facts and, via analysis, to resolution/conclusion. A form of rationalizing that can ignore the meaning-rich power of non-Western (non-logo-centric) language forms. This can be dramatically illustrated in Benjamin Lee Whorf's description of the Hopi Indian language, as being comparable to English as the 'rapier to a bludgeon' – a radically different way to describe (and so constitute) Reality; especially in relation to metaphysics; so opening access to finely drawn imaginative ideas. A number of recent post-modern continental philosophers, notably Jacques Derrida, have drawn attention to this prioritising of log-centrism in traditional Western philosophy, if without suggesting a convincing alternative.

Which only realistically leaves us into seeing at least some potential value in taking an openly rational approach to conflictual issues, but retaining a preparedness to reformulate the conditions of the rational as a result of experience or of insights drawn from non-logo-centric sources.

Rational processes that involve: clarity of definitions, a coherent form of setting out arguments or views, consistency in ideas, and a willingness to consider criticisms within a more general recursive process of authorial self-examination This last can relate to non logo-centric considerations, and is potentially a key source of redefining the rational process itself if, that is, this process is designed to evermore effectively access Reality and translate its implications into knowledge. Even with his illuminating qualifications, I don't think that Derrida would deny at least some residue of genuine interpretive value in the application of some aspects of rationalism – providing we accept the limitations.

Our enculturalization enwraps us in forms of language regularizing a particular grammatical structure, appropriate phonemic forms, and the use of certain metaphors and analogies, all within an assumed usage. It is difficult to examine the constitution of the wrappings of our 'natural' language if we only have that language itself with which to do so. And yet, critical analysis informed by an understanding of the potential constraints of our language, and perhaps a genuine openness to other language forms, can stimulate our imagination and widen our conceptual horizons even to the point of exposing the '.....vertinginous prospects henceforth opened up for inventive reading.' As noted by Christopher Norris in his 1987 book.

In the course of this essay I have moved from an outline of some of the history of philosophical speculation and suggested it to represent a vast, potentially valuable, reservoir of reasoned imagination that is our intellectual heritage. It globally encompasses the work of so many individuals attempting to share their considered reflections on aspects of their 'encounter within Being'. I then moved on to speculate upon this encounter from my own perspective, including certain presuppositions. I stated my purpose as being to create concepts that relate closely to actual lived experience, a lived experience that has been problematic for the human species, especially in relation to evil. But I admit that my concepts can be prone to semantic bagginess, indeed even vagueness, as I endeavour to find a balance between linguistic precision and explanatory scope – I would hope that the value of the latter goes at least some way to allow for the imprecision. I posit heuristic concepts (rather than 'truths') that I assume to be of use in understanding aspects of the 'human condition'.

In order to begin I synthetically separated three aspects of humankind's thinking process, those of Reality - Language - Thought, and considered each of them in turn, highlighting what I consider to be their most significant characteristics. I then re-united these into the wholeness in which they belong within the unity of human thought/existence (as embodied in subjectivities). I invoked the atomic concepts of sign and of sign-situations, as the starting point for any consideration of the experience of be-ing. Sign-situations as being the fluid unity of associated signs contained within relatively integrated symbol systems, having the potential to expand as any issue/event develops. Next I introduced the concepts of mean-ing and understanding as the means by which we gain access to, and interpret, Reality. Three more concepts, intentionality, perspective, and provisionalism, were posited to complete my descriptive outline of the structure of thinking. This then exposed a significant contributory cause for intra and inter personal, group, national, and other types of conflict. Conflicts wherein 'evil' can be so easily expressed. Having exposed the most basic cause of conflict, finding it, – differential perspective-taking - to be deeply rooted in the human condition, we can focus on possible ways of resolving or reducing conflict.

Throughout my more descriptive analysis I have endeavoured to trace the formative paths of the semantic substance expressed in some of my concepts and found the trail divided, with one path leading down into our organicity, and the other leading up towards the raised understanding of existence (the proto-transcendental) that continuing bio become social become civil evolution potentially offers. I have made myself liable to the accusation of a type of 'naturalism' whereby in an intellectually deterministic way when, owing to my intellectual shortcomings, I appear to seek comfort in an easy organic base, as a 'touch stone' to always come back to, in which to find a deceptive form of intellectual solace. In defence, since my late teens I have been driven by the need to understand the human condition for its own sake, I wanted to know how and why and under what conditions we have life (a unique window on self-consciousness), and also what were the causes of so much evil in the World. For around 40 years I have, in order to progress the search for the satisfaction of these needs and guided by them, studied in depth and in breadth across relevant areas of humankind's intellectual and religious endeavour. A conclusion I feel most confident about is that in some complicated way, for reasons unknown, human beings have evolved from ever lower life-forms over billions of years, and that this evolution, originally electro/chemical, then overlying these biological, then overlying these socio/cultural (each mode being subsumed within the 'higher' mode) is a continuing process. Within this evolutionary development can be identified a progression of organic forms able to process evermore complex information, with self-conscious human beings currently representing the known apex of this progression.

Confidence in the conclusions of any analysis can only ever stand on the foundations of 'faith', but a faith underpinned by a trust in the soundness and intellectual integrity of one's procedures (integrity of the associated reasoning), rather than the type of faith which underpins the dogmatic certainty of all religionists and most ideologues. Meaning inheres within our organicity, even if human cognitive ability provides the means to form a mode of awareness we would term 'understanding'; an outcome of a conceived semantic unity allowing us to make sense of an experience. This being a level of awareness that provides the psychological conditions to stimulate suitable adaptive behaviours, so functionally directed, but also for us to stimulate more reflective abstract thought patterns.

In my view such was the value of taking an evolutionary (organic) perspective to the understanding of the human condition that I started with it as a presumption rather than pretending to arrive at it as a conclusion.

There is an associated implication of accepting an evolutionary perspective, one that involves the future of humankind. It seems that social/cultural evolution has provided us as a species with the ability to overcome such threats as are faced by other species, we can use technology to insulate us (as a species), at least to some considerable extent, from biological dangers. Whether it's that of predatory animals, species threatening disease, or threats to food supplies. But longer-term evolutionary 'choices' for any species are limited - A species can continue a process of adaptive change, developing in ways (mutational and/or behavioural) conducive to new species formation e.g. some form of earlier Homo (H.habilis, H.erectus, or H.heidelbergensis) to Homo sapien circa 100,000 y.b.p. - Can become 'fixed' and remain stable as a species for 100s of millions of years e.g. alligator, tortoise, dragonfly - Can find itself in a habitat that, due to dramatic change in its environmental conditions, it is unable to adapt and so becomes extinct e.g. the large-bodied dinosaurs circa 65 m.y.b.p. (following a period of ascendancy lasting for over 160 million years). And even some species of Homo who have left but a fossil record of their specific existence e.g. Homo neanderthal and Homo denisovan – if also some measure of genetic inheritance gifted to Homo sapien.

One of these will happen to our species even given the 'information processing' advances made by bio-social-civil evolution. I think that the choice is between the first (species change) and the last (extinction). But unlike any other species that has taken one of the three evolutionary paths the introduction of socio/cultural factors, with the corresponding ability to control and destroy, means that the path taken by humankind lies to a considerable extent, in its own hands.

I need to emphasize that when I refer to evolution it is not biological evolution as usually understood. I want to highlight the progressive development of organisms, in terms of their ability to process information, from 'pre-conscious' organisms to 'self-conscious' human beings. The loosely definable stages being – autonomous self-replicating molecular chains - simple cellular organisms only able to process information related to the maintenance of a simple homeostatic balance (e.g. bacteria, paramecium, amoeba) - a biologically pre-conscious organism, distinctly multi-cellular, with cell differentiation forming simple organs within the body, and a distinct information processing mechanism centred on a primitive nervous system with a notochord enlarged at the anterior end (e.g. acorn-worms, amphioxus, nematodes). The information processing mechanisms then become rather more complicated and, with the appearance and development of modes of consciousness, the species of animals involved are best understood at representing a range of consciousness with four clearly identifiable types as embodied in fish, reptiles, non-primate mammals, and primate mammals. Considered simplistically, the first three types possessing an 'awareness' of only their more immediate environments, without any evidence of conscious memories based on reflection. With fish and reptiles exhibiting fixed behaviours in terms of reflexes and innate learning patterns invoked by environmental stimuli. But with non-primate mammals exhibiting more flexible behaviours, an ability to learn in adapting to changing aspects of their environment, and with most species behaving in ways that we would term 'social'. Features of their information processing ability that has led humans to tame and domesticate members of some of the more advanced (in information processing terms) species.

With the primate mammals, these divide into non-human and human primates, the former definitely conscious with features of very limited self-consciousness, including the ability to learn fairly simple behaviours, to 'hold' new information in consciousness for short periods, to interact on simple to quite complex social levels, and to exhibit limited cognitive ability e.g. a chimpanzee using a box and a stick to reach some bananas. Interestingly, they also exhibit within-species emotions such as jealousy, long-term dislike or attachment to group members, and unhappiness or sadness. This is not simply inappropriate anthropomorphism but clear, well-studied, features of non-

122

human primate behaviour.

When we come to 'human' primates, we again find a range of cognitive abilities (cognitive as compared with biological/organic and more emotion-based and pre, or only proto, linguistic information processing) as expressed by the different species of homo, taking forms that bridge the information processing range, between non-human and modern human primates.

One 'marker' that has been identified as expressing cognitive ability (reflective information processing) is that of 'tool-making', and a traceable line of development in tool-making can be followed in the overlapping but sequential duration of the various hominin (especially Homo) species living from circa 2.5 m.y.b.p. With these species - all but Homo sapien having become extinct - we see the progressive development of self-consciousness in advance of any other species. Self-consciousness in Homo sapien fully aware of itself as a be-ing within a relationship to what is experienced as an external environment separate from itself. Possessing an accessible memory and able to imagine and plan possible futures, with a symbol system (realized in images, expressed emotions, and in language in its widest sense) allowing the re-presentation of information which has led to highly complex scientific and technological advances, to cities, space-craft, the media, mechanised food production, medical-related technological developments, and the means of techno-warfare including nuclear and biological weapons, all the lethal so-called conventional weaponry, as well as imaginative philosophical speculation encompassing both formal philosophies and more traditional sources of wisdom.

These developments illustrate the presence of contradictory forces within the self-conscious psyche, most of which can make one pessimistic about which of the three 'choices' already noted will be made by the human species. But a close consideration of how evolution operates, the way that socio/cultural factors have greatly accelerated this process, and a little imaginative optimism, allows the possibility of a different choice (a more positive future) being open to our species.

Self-consciousness in humans can be distinguished from the self-awareness exhibited by other advanced primates in the capacity we have for 'reflection', the extent that we can hold ideas before the mind and follow-up the implications of these – an ability dependent on a memory capacity and projective imagination significantly beyond those of any other primate species.

I want to draw attention to a role (use) for language in representing the mutational material upon which a form of adaptive selection operates – if not the seemingly more singular form of mutations that characterise genetic mutation.

Earlier in the essay I noted the study of metaphysics (philosophical speculation) as a 'growth-bud' of our species information-processing based evolutionary development...... especially the questing into the elusive essence of Being. This quest is inextricably linked to conceptual thinking and to language more generally, and I want to suggest an admittedly highly speculative analogy between genetic mutation and language (and associated cognitive) change as each being essential aspects of the information processing dynamic underlying evolutionary development and the idea of 'mutation' – both being mechanisms for processing complex information. The genetic-based change noted as mutation (replication 'error') is biochemical (coding for the production of proteins) and linguistic/conceptual-based change is a form of semantic/semiotic mutation. I am not sure what would be the equivalent 'coding mechanism' of linguistic/conceptual replication (other than language itself) - possibly phonemes - and the mechanism for change (equivalent to bio-chemical mutation in genes) is more a diffuse form of 'mutation' by accumulation. But if we consider the changes taking place in life on earth over the past 3.8 billon years we can quite easily identify when significantly new modes of information process (the evolution of consciousness) arise.

I think that the underlying principle of this language-mutation by accumulation idea can be compared to Richard Dawkins original idea of 'memes', and Daniel Dennett's and Susan Blackmore's individual versions of these.

For these three 'memes' are discrete patterns of information e.g. an idea, an invention, a artistic/architectural technique, a joke, an idea that goes 'viral' on the internet. These memes can be horizontally and vertically transmitted between peoples by imitation/learning and being replicated through generations (Dennett suggests memes as being 'virus-like'). They are cultural artefacts that can change ('mutate') during the process of replication/transmission. I assume that an example could be the description of how the solar system operates could be a 'meme'. With the earth-centric version of the meme conceding to the Copernican sun-centred version due to changing ('mutated') information content. So, similar to genetic replication/transmission, information-based memetic entities are also liable to change in the process of replicating.

With memes constituted by such entities as: 'ideas', 'phrases', 'slogans', 'tunes', 'songs' and similar discrete packages of information, rather than a specific coding mechanism, for cultural 'evolution' (or to explain cultural development). Minds generate memes and minds are psychological platforms/spaces for meme transmission. For Dennett and Blackmore some meme propagation mechanism underlies the physiological evolution of the brain itself. Dennett's emphasis is on words as memes, but I assume he means words as a medium for mimetic transmission (a word in itself can hardly be a 'meme' – some meaning related context is required).

A possible criticism of the comparison between genes and memes being the lack of any equivalent 'codons' (a 'code-script') for memes. I think this is probably a valid criticism, but a sophisticated description of the role of 'phonemes' in language and the ways in which these have developed over the last 100,000 years could offer something useful here. Each gene in DNA has three codons (a triplet base) composed of three of four types of nucleo bases, and transmission is based on replication of patterns of these; a nicely coherent bio-mechanism with replication errors constituting the mutations (and a process of natural selection retaining the most functionally 'useful' – as in promotes reproductive success - in any population). Whereas memes seem to lack any clear structural (biological or even conceptual) mechanism. But as an idea they do stimulate thinking of how social/cultural change occurs. If we reverse engineer human cultural (especially scientific) achievements of today it does seem probable that some more discrete mechanism for change might lie within human psychological/thinking processes. Processes, the products of which are transmissible and liable to change.

Please view my own linguistic/cognition based 'mutation' analogy as simply being my seeking to highlight the role of language as the more obvious probing adaptational growth-tip of humankind's awareness of its own presence within Being. My type of mutation-by-accumulation is interlinked with consciousness (levels of awareness) so closely linked to cognition. This is not language as social communication which is more circular, and in that sense uncreative; sustaining adaptation rather than progressing its advance. In relation to adaptive potential, language has the potential to facilitate the investigation of the unexplored terrain of the metaphysical, can perhaps allow us to adapt in ways which can advance the very horizon of our understanding of our be-ing.

It does seem that memes as cultural artefacts, and my suggestion of some form of interlinked linguistic/cognitive development, both highlight ongoing evolutionary development – if more obviously about creation of novel information than biological adaptation. The Dawkins/Dennett/Blackmore memes are just noted more as observations on evolving cultural practices (with unknown outcomes – the dynamic being their own intentions to multiply and 'spread' within a population – the 'selfish meme' to complement the 'selfish gene' posited by Dawkins) rather than in terms of progressive evolutionary implications for consciousness itself. Dennett and Blackmore do suggest co-evolutionary changes (involving gene-meme interaction) in brain physiology but without noting the implications for the evolution of consciousness itself. The concept of meme seems to be limited to the circumscription of such cultural artefacts (and so semantic substance) as identifiable technological, scientific, artistic, religious, philosophical, political, and those retained in popular culture, etc. ideas and other types of cultural progression within the mode of self-consciousness (I do understand their academic reluctance to go further). Whereas my own idea (unhampered by much pretence at academic status) implies a progression towards a new mode of consciousness beyond today's mode of self-consciousness, and so perhaps some useful potential for probing further into the metaphysical; especially the aspect of this that involves Being.

If not occurring randomly as genetic mutation seems to be, the replication changes in my own idea of the evolution of consciousness are about following a more progressive accumulation of related information leading to an obvious semantic difference between the original and the replicated idea. The dynamic for this progression being the fundamental evolutionary fact of the creation of organisms that can process and generate ever more complex information. So in this sense teleological, if one seemingly blind as to what this really means/implies for our be-ing.

Genetic mutations in isolation do not necessarily lead to a significant improvement in an organism's ability to adapt (so enhancing reproductive potential), genetic mutations accumulate prior to any clear behavioural change appears. Think of the human eye, its very complexity involves 0000s of mutations that contributed, over about 600 million years, to a progression from the light sensitive patches (of photo-receptive protein molecules) of single-celled organisms (the 'eye-spots') that evolved in stages of complexification for light sensitivity, shape and movement detection, colour vision, to the full consciousness of primate 'sight'. With the small bundles of light sensitive molecules, over million years of evolutionary development, becoming the human eye with its each complex biological components – primary ones being…sclera, cornea, iris, lens, pupil, retina, the tissue-like cells of the vitreous humour and the intricate weave of tiny blood vessels that sustain all of these; and this without even considering the complex neural connections within the central and peripheral nervous systems – all operating to form what we call 'sight'. Just consider the many thousands of genetic mutations that this process must have involved, if one 'driven' by the significant adaptational advantage that organisms/creatures with sight (and improvements on this within species) would have in the process of natural selection. Light sensitivity would have significantly enlarged an organism's ability to adapt. And the evolving 'eye' would have led to an increasingly more expansive harvesting of perceptual information, with primate sight leading to an acceleration of adaptational ability. For humans, what technological inventions or scientific discoveries would have been possible without 'sight' (although of course blind and partially sighted individuals would no doubt have made contributions to some of these) both the outwardly directed experience of the external world, and for most people an inner sense linked to sight allowing thought to be experienced as images. In the evolution of the 'eye' we can see the progressive enhancement of the amount and complexity of information available to be processed. So we can understand how linguistic/cognitive evolution would also be accumulative with innovation in information species processing ability only being identified over million-year timespans.

A problem I have in expressing what I mean is that I do not know the psychological form that the next successful evolutionary mode will take. Only the assumption that it will advance the information processing dynamic – but it would surely be in a form of 'transcendental awareness'. Awareness being a blend of a sense of being physically present in the world and a sense of an inner self processing information; these being the primary elements of consciousness. Elsewhere I have used the term 'world-consciousness' to express this future mode of enhanced awareness; this being a marked development of the current mode of 'self-consciousness' which in human form was a progression on the types of 'consciousness' exhibited by non-human primates. Given this ignorance of what type of metaphysical outline would allow the successful probing into Being, I can only make suggestions based more on projections on the known past experience of humankind, and its more immediate primate ancestor.

Think of a Homo species of around two million years ago, say Homo heidelbergensis (brain capacity of about 1200cc, modern humans about 1400cc) – tool makers and uses.............what were the cognitive (concept generating) dimensions of their psychology? Was there sufficient emotional space, and a level of cognitive capacity, for some reflective sense of an unknown beyond the immediacies of life, or was their psychological world limited to a focus on the social, their 'proto-language' only for communication (it has been suggested that the capacity for more articulated speech only evolved circa 500 t.y.b.p. - see R. Dunbar, 2014).

Tools and the multiplicity of other cultural artefacts made from about 2.5 m.y.b.p. onwards provide evidence of developing self-consciousness; of a rising level of awareness. Homo sapiens emerged very roughly from 150 t.y.b.p., with a modern type from about 50 t.y.b.p. What would have been the metaphysical ideas of the early form of humankind? Grave goods and various forms of artworks from 50-30 t.y.b.p. more obviously suggest an easy ability to abstract from the immediate in quite imaginative ways. But I think it is fair to assume (on what evidence, and fair extrapolation from this, can reasonably allow) that this creature's relatively expansive cognitive ability would have been focused on applying this in novel ways to control the environment and perhaps to maintaining more formally structured social hierarchies (arrangements) within groups. Any psychological space (of early Homo sapien) for what we might term metaphysical speculation would probably have been channelled into natural religions/totemisms; ones populated with ancestors and mythical creatures, and interpreting landscapes, animals, and immediate locations as being infused with the spiritual. In terms of written material, it is with the early Greek philosophers that the foundations for Western metaphysics were laid down. Foundations upon which a range of systems, and the rational methods of formulating these, have developed. Metaphysicians (across the world) have endeavoured to realize the conditions necessary to peer beyond the horizon of human understanding - to transcend our mundane conceptual boundary within Reality and so to at least potentially advance this – We might consider that little progress has been made in nearly five thousand years of civil life......but stand back and consider the last 50,000, 100,000, 1,000,000 years? Just imagine the different conceptual outlook (in term of metaphysical questions) of even an early modern Homo (circa 50,000 y.b.p.) with that of Plato, Aristotle, Descartes, Kant, Hegel, Husserl, Whitehead, Pierce, as more systematic metaphysicians, and the somewhat fragmented but some still innovative more metaphysical philosophers of the late 20th and early 21st centuries.

We cannot predict what will be the case in terms of metaphysical questions in even just the next 50,000 years – What can we know? – What should we do? – What can we hope? And underlying these, our species relationship to Being. But I think that our evolutionary become historical past allows us to infer that the suggested answers could be quite different from those currently on offer – and it is evolving (conceptually and so imaginatively 'mutating') language and associated cognitive developments that are taking us towards a condition that will necessarily be beyond the limitations of self-consciousness as a mode of information processing.

So this digression into evolution as it relates to metaphysics is intended to offer some chronological context, and tentative reason, why so many different systems (and the justification for rejecting such systems) have been devised. Over 2,600 thousand years of metaphysical philosophising seems merely to have articulated our ignorance. But in doing so it has significantly expanded humankind's conceptual toolkit and imaginative outlook. And the same source of curiosity has no doubt generated the technology, the sciences, and stimulated the arts.

In sum: our evolutionary past suggests exciting prospects for our future intellectual development if, that is, our species survives present times.

Having earlier attempted to outline the general structure of the human 'thinking' condition, as but a heuristic exercise in description, we can identify differential perspective-taking as the intentional source for the expression of evil. Is this just noting the obvious admission of our taking different, sometimes conflictual, views on any issue? In a more immediate sense yes, but introducing the concept of differential perspective taking is intended to highlight the processes providing the formative constitution of a person's perspective; and by extension the shared perspective of a group such as a religion, tribe, political or ethnic grouping, economic class, or a nation.

I suggest that this intra-subjectivity (usually within a range of views – perhaps adjusting to maintain some sense of personal or group consistency) reflects a constituting fluidity that could also serve to form the basis of resolving conflicts. Perspectives are malleable and can potentially change due to new information becoming available or to current information being subject to reconsideration. And of course 'reason' could provide the negotiational terminology (and intellectual pre-conditions) for any process endeavouring to achieve resolution, or at least some conditional agreement on containment, of an issue.

More serious conflicts feature in three primary areas – interpersonal relationships – philosophical disagreement – group (e.g. religious, ethnic, national) conflict.

The form of disagreement in interpersonal relationships is often dependent on the 'power' resources available to each of the individuals involved; power that can be explicit such as economic dependency or assumed religious injunctions, or implicit such as emotional dependency or social expectations. Failure of successful 'negotiation' (whether admittance of responsibility, agreement on a compromise, reluctant concessions, etc.) can result in residual antagonism or complete relationship breakdown – outcomes that can have a significant impact on the individuals directly involved and on connected relationships involving children of antagonistic parents or brothers, sisters, and parents, of antagonistic siblings. But in terms of the expression of evil, the worst outcomes of these – if possibly quite dramatically life-changing for individuals - would almost always have only a local, relatively small-scale, impact.

If philosophical disagreements create hardly a ripple of interest in the 'real world' they do illustrate how even well-founded reasoning processes can, in the realm of conceptual abstractions and the reality of linguistic fluidity (fuzziness), lead to markedly different perspectives. I have also suggested that philosophical disagreement over metaphysical forms and issues could link to aspects of human evolution and our species future.

The principle philosophical frameworks, the 'isms', are broadly labelled as: empiricism, idealism, phenomenology, pragmatism, logical positivism, analytic philosophy, existentialism, structuralism, modernism and related more post-modern approaches. They each begin with certain different primary assumptions about our experience and so it is unsurprising that even quite, at times forensically, consistent reasoning leads to markedly different outcomes. Most obviously apparent in areas such as: determinism/freewill, the constitutional nature of Reality, subject/objective, mind/matter, the critical consideration of language use, and the nature of

131

truth. Again, as with personal relationships, the realm of philosophy disagreements cause little open conflict, indeed they can serve as a fertile resource to generate a seemingly endless stream of PhDs. But when philosophical frameworks are adapted to support ideologies they can appear to offer some intellectual credibility for the most spurious ideas.

In terms of the primary consideration of this essay, the question of evil, it is disagreement at the group (tribe, religion, ethnicity, nation,) levels that elevates the crucial experiential fault-line in the human condition onto another, a species-critical, level. A fault-line whose sources can be revealed by an examination of the intentional substructure underlying differential perspective-taking for each circumscribed issue where evil is expressed. With this fracture being elevated to species critical due primarily to four issues confronting humanity:

Global issues:

- Increasingly unsustainable environmental conditions

- Threatened or actual armed conflict (even to the point of nuclear war), both between nations and within nations as civil wars – set off by competition over valued resources such as: water, land, fossil fuels, rare and valued metals and minerals, power, and knowledge. Examples of which can be seen throughout much of the world just now.

- Who will control artificial intelligence.

- The outcomes of gross, and increasing, income and wealth inequality; more especially economic poverty.

What is required if we are to design global institutional structures that will reconstruct the world in the form of a 'home' for humanity rather than various terrains of contestation in which the powerful relentlessly emerge victorious and the poor and defenceless relentlessly suffer:

- The innovative skills of scientists......tasked with a purpose.

- The analytic skills of philosophers.......tasked with a purpose.

- The wisdom of leaders unfettered by personal ambition...... tasked with outlining a purpose focused on the four Global issues noted above, and of designing institutions of governance suitable for addressing these.

And of course, the actual engagement of mass populations as a necessary pre-condition to stimulate and sustain the requirements just noted.

Conclusion

Much of the next few pages are an edited version of a section in the concluding chapter of a previous book (Dyer, 2021).

I have been endeavouring to outline the conditions of our experience within Reality and how this links to the expression of evil in civil history and around the world today. And my giving priority to the concept of authenticity as an existential aspiration is intended to express some deeper connection to all the potential good that inheres within the human condition. Authenticity as a form of transcendent achievement realized as an outcome of a mode of world-consciously directed engagement with life. The lived outcome of a decision to assume a fundamental level of personal responsibility for the implications of the mystery of finding oneself in existence. The question authentic in relation to what stands out.... bear with me.

I have traced the rise of consciousness in terms of the increasing potential to process information and I point to human self-consciousness as being an advanced embodiment of this ability. Human history shows that the gross expression of evil has been a fearsome and bleak feature running throughout the social processes and cultural institutions that have characterized civilizations associated with self-consciousness. But another aspect of civil life has been the refinement of morality, given a symbolic and ordered form in scriptural commands, civil laws (codes - injunctions) and in stated aims informed by enlightened humanistic aspirations. In relation to these types of codified ethical considerations - in the context of 'world consciousness' - we now have various human rights acts and I would highlight the UN's collective version of these as set out in its charter; an embodiment of hope for the human species. (see Appendix below)

A problem for any individual setting out to confront evil today being the disjunction between action at the personal and local levels, and action at the national and global levels. We can at least attempt to resolve this challenge by, as individuals, reflecting and then deciding upon a realistic action-based balance in our lives, but a balance rooted in authenticity, and emerging from a morality based upon world-conscious values.

Foucault, commenting on the responsibility and possibility of authentic self-hood in his 'Politics of Truth' (1997 ed, p158), recommend the night-time practice followed by Seneca ('De Ira') who writes of conducting: '.....an inquest on one's day? What sleep better than that which follows this review of one's action. How calm it is, deep and free, when the soul has received its portion of praise and blame, and has submitted itself to its own examination, its own censure. Secretly, it makes the trial of its own conduct. I exercise this authority over myself as witness before myself........I hide nothing from myself; I spare myself nothing.'

A daily opportunity for the more reflexive consideration of one's life - not some introverted religious contemplation clinging to a self-seeking relationship to a god - not some calculating daily audit on progress towards the achievement of personal material ambitions - but instead, a proactive time located at the end of each day, a time when quietude, and a mode of intense solitary contemplation offers an opportunity for personal life to be considered; the potentially creative opportunity to form an individual's decided ethical stance towards life, and lived truth, in which coheres tomorrow's possibilities. It is within this intimate process of personal reflection and decision-making that the resources for authenticity inhere. But it does require some thought-through sense of an appropriate life – of values against which aspirations and behaviour are to be judged.

From where does this set of values arise? Foucault (ibid, p156) writes of an: 'hermeneutics of the self' with reference to the ancient Greek Delphic injunction to 'know thyself', set in the wider context of historical processes when at a later time medieval institutions of Christianity and Islam offered an unsatisfactory change in the methodology of self-examination by promoting faith over personal responsibility for others.

But I think we could also view this expression ('hermeneutics of the self') as indicating an interpretative boundary between how we do live and how we might formulate the ways in which we should live – reimagining the possible from the actual.

The claim that the 'unexamined life isn't worth living' is, in itself a value judgment – the question 'why' stands out. But if we are prepared to rigorously consider the implications of following such an injunction to progress a reflective process of considering the conditions of our lives it becomes a more substantial statement; indeed it offers a direct challenge to our sense of personal autonomy.

Any exercise in progressive revelation should not be just some introspective indulgence seeking to peel off layers of personality to expose some 'real' kernel of personhood that the detritus of everyday concerns and distractions have overlain. Of discovering some deep-seated self that has long been present but only in the form of a nascent presence. Rather, the exercise is more about accomplishment in the sense of being a self-creative revealing of what you might become.

Whilst I would concede that religion continues to play an important support role in the lives of many individuals, the decision to live with the ethical implications of a world conscious level of awareness must be a very personal one - each of us prepared to stand fully exposed to the corscourating blast of lived reality – combining together in action, but to do so as autonomous moral agents fostering the changes, incremental and revolutionary, that can contribute to the construction of a fairer, less evil, world. The emotional and cognitive resources – religious or secular - that we each draw upon matters less than accepting that the outcome is our own responsibility. Indeed doing so sets the parameters within which our authenticity can be defined.

In terms of understanding the world and interacting with others – of social living - self-consciousness tends towards a narrowing of view, primarily linked to personal and group interests. Self-consciousness tends towards seeing the other as friend or foe, and the foe usually being the unknown other. Self-consciousness tends towards stereotypic categorization of others, tends to notice difference rather than underlying sameness, self-consciousness at home in a post-industrial consumer society tends towards a focus on self rather than on common interests. Tends towards reductionist thinking; if not the reductionist analysis of the sciences - more the silo-like narrowing of, me, myself, and of my family, my tribe or group, my nation.......my 'kind', rather than more holistic worldly thinking. Generally a repressive tendency towards essentialist and stereotypic thinking, of reducing issues to simplistic explanations often sanctioned by tradition and, in a post-modern mass society of accepting the interpretations of experts and other influential individuals whose views have a more general coherence with an individual's own intentionality; basically a tendency towards intellectual laziness and therefore an outlook that mitigates against much personal commitment to the clarification of moral issues and their implications. Note my repeated use of the word 'tends', this indicates that the characteristics I am describing express core aspects of self-consciousness, but that at anytime aspects of our next evolutionary stage, 'world-consciousness', can intrude. We can rise above the limitation of a narrow self-consciousness; tendencies can be resisted.

It is this originating, personally interpretive, aspect of our experience that offers hope for change. This capacity for creative agency (allied to an aspirational human imagination) offers the basic psychological conditions for the construction of social, economic, and political systems that can provide some humanity-affirming structures, and so is our hope for humanity.

Being human in its-self not a pathological condition - The uniqueness of individuality is a fundamental opportunity to 'be'. For some this being is in suffering, for others in creative becoming, and for most being in a more mundane sense from which we can each seek to progressively develop our own level of consciousness.

Given the serious and sombre threats of nuclear destruction, environmental disaster, domination by A.I., and extreme asymmetries of wealth and power, facing the word today, people whose lives are not constrained by the immediacies of poverty and whose primary concern is not in endeavouring to eke out a living on a daily basis, have a responsibility to determine revolutionary change......but then how can building a world freed from the threat of species catastrophe, and a world in which economic fairness pertains, be revolutionary? Isn't it more about necessary rather than revolutionary change?

How do we as individuals deal with the global problems that seem to be beyond any of us in a world whose civil institutions have been constructed by historical circumstances, a world now controlled by national and transnational elites? To begin we, each one of us, needs the 'courage to be', not in the sense of the media-debased currency of overinflated heroism, but rather to garner the courage that would allow us to realize the potential to be fully human in our lives - to carry a sense of world-consciousness and an awareness of how this, more transcendental perspective, relates to our daily lives. The courage to stand against injustice, against economic exploitation and social discrimination; against the everyday evils we might chose to pass by being suffered by those that it is convenient to not see - where we rationalize our reluctance to engage.

For us to more comfortably adopt the vernacular of humanistic values, and to establish frameworks of solidarity that encompass the dispossessed, the socially repressed, and the economically exploited. The courage to take responsibility for lives lived as workers, as consumers, as neighbours, as friends, and as citizens of the more powerful civil societies. Aspiring to world-consciousness would enable each of us to transcend self-consciousness - to connect with the evolutionary potential inherent, if only for now as a possibility, in our species.

A difficulty in realizing the constitutive element of courage is to feel that we can be effective - in a world whose institutions are constructed to make us feel discouraged, politically neutered, distracted by entertainment and other forms of wants-based consumerism, and so to be obediently managed. We need to establish and support forums where we can share concerns, reinforce current and create new connections, and build a global sense of common purpose and these at the local, regional, national, and transnational levels. To build a mutually supportive conspiracy of liberation against the forces of control that we must stand against. A conspiracy initially fostered in our own hearts but one forming and using local, national, and international, connective links, not least those made possible by the internet, to promote and sustain global action. We, each of us, seeking to eschew the everyday accommodations and compromises we might make with obvious injustice.

As individuals, we can either obediently align our lives with pathways that unquestionably accept the normalized relativities of our home society, or we could engage with the world in a significantly different way. To endeavour to use analytic ability and imagination to mentally 'step outside' of the established patterns of our lives - this is the fundamental choice we each have to make. Developing the stance we take to the world following thoroughgoing analysis of central aspects of our lives. It would involve a type of loneliness (or rather 'alone-ness') if we do seek to break free of socialized behaviour patterns; especially if these involve an orthodox religious or politically conservative background. Bear in mind that I am not suggesting rejection, the discarding, of what we have come to accept, but accepting it on relativised terms and aspiring to transcend this relativity.

Each one of us has at least some tenuous hold on kindness, can be in touch with our humanity. Life-denying, cruel and violent upbringings - the child solider, the bullied or battered child, the baby deprived of adequate nutrition, early exposure to religious fundamentalism or relentless racism - can understandably leave a child or adult deficient in the ability to feel empathy towards others, but for most the potential to do good rather than accept evil is irredeemably present within the depth of our personality. Even those many psychologically wounded, so socially dysfunctional, victims brought up in dehumanizing circumstances might be redeemed with a sufficiency of care, and appropriate support.

We, as individuals, are born within a Reality of which we

come to be both confronted with in the sense of having to negotiate our passing through it as well as being within it as a uniquely creative dimension. It confronts and yet includes ourselves; an inextricable relationship gaining a dynamic element from its ever-expanding experiential content. I have posited Reality as all that there is; no string of descriptors, whether adjectival, adverbial, or even numerical, can capture the profound sense of just what this means.

If information is the medium of the Universe (when energy and mass are the substance, and space-time allows for their expression), then the evolutionary story has been about the appearance of organisms with constitutions that enable an ever-increasing capacity to process information as the primary bio-mechanism driving species adaptation and radiation.

Immanuel Kant noted his wonder at: 'The starry heavens above me and the moral law within me......I see them before me and connect them immediately with the consciousness of my existence.'

This short phrase encapsulates the core aspects of humanity at its best – driven by curiosity to explore the out-there and challenged by our conscience to consider the moral implications of our lives.

Earlier in this text I noted how we 'find ourselves in existence', doing so in order to express the perspective of a meta-awareness whereby we can view the relativity of our particular situations within a nexus of pre-established relationships and social institutions, and also realising the uniqueness of each of our own experientially formed perspective on life. This perspective can include an awareness of our being present on a ecologically fragile blue/green planet spinning lazily on its axis as it traverses an elliptical passage around the more substantial Sun. These two bodies of the Solar System providing the material means to sustain humankind's journey through time. Echoing Kant ....allowing us to gaze with curious wonder upon the starry skies – and for our imaginations to roam through our lived experience, forming ideas of the possible.

The suggestion that we 'find ourselves' within existence – implies the finding of the already there as well as the realization that most of us have the agency to transcend the limitations of the socialization processes that we have experienced.

The responsibility we have as individuals, if we commit to foster 'world consciousness' within ourselves and in our relations to others, is for us to endeavour to understand the world we find ourselves within and then to seek to move beyond our more local (national, interest-group, religion, tribe, ideology, etc.) interests to ones more likely to improve global conditions for all of its seven billion and rising number of people – both in basic material conditions and for all to be able to experience some 'peace of mind' for their lives and those of their children, grandchildren, and the generations that we hope will follow.

I am suggesting that we have an existential responsibility to purposefully decide on how we should live, not in term of personal career, close relationships, day to day attitudes, etc (although these would also probably come to be involved) but a deeper level of considering our lives in the context of humanity itself rather than the individual as myself.

There is a correspondence between perspective-taking on your own life within Reality in terms of self-creative engagement with a future involving others – the cognitive bridge to world-consciousness - and the key task of endeavoring to 'take-up' the perspective of others in relation to this situation or that issue. Each requires us to adopt processes determined to transcend two aspects of our individuality, the first the individual as socialized, the second as an individual prepared to assume a level of social responsibility beyond their more immediate relationships; and each of these as processes of open-ended engagement. Both directed towards transcendence – moving beyond the narrowness of the accidentally socialized and of the self-centring tendencies of self-consciousness.

Life (be-ing) within Being is a ontologically mysterious experience, aspects of the condition being poetically phrased by Blaize Pascal when he wrote: *'When I consider the short duration of my life, swallowed up in the eternity of before and after, the little space which I fill, and even can see, engulfed in the infinite immensity of spaces of which I am ignorant, and which know me not, I am frightened and am astonished at being here rather than there; for there is no reason why here rather than there, why now rather than then......The eternal silence of these infinite spaces frightens me.'* (Taken from Theodosius Dobzhansky, 1976, p346).

Within this quote we can realize both the insignificance '......swallowed up in the eternity...' but also our uniqueness '.....why here rather than there, why now rather than then....' And it is within this uniqueness that lies not only the responsibility to contribute to humankind's evolutionary potential but also our chance to step forward and live moral lives even in the recognition of life's seeming absurdity. The last being perhaps the hardest most personally autonomous decision – an existential conundrum to be faced or avoided but always there as a brooding presence in our lives.

Possibly the boldest action we can each take as an individual is to question ourselves in the world – to create personal authenticity out of deep, open, reflection. Authentic as being self-created in terms of both: our own interior lives to develop a reflexive, if critical, interpretive mode for our experience and also how we become externally directed towards the world. In order to gain these facets of authenticated self-hood you would have worked through the central implications of 'finding oneself within existence'. And this by a consideration of your genealogical connection to the evolutionary, become civil, heritage of our species and of your more immediate connection to the present as a citizen of the world.

This is a sombre responsibility, but surely also the most creative grasping of freedom for each of us to Be and so to Become. To Become........entangled with human truth and our human future.

APPENDIX

PROPOSALS FOR THE ESTABLISHMENT OF A GENERAL INTERNATIONAL ORGANIZATION [1]

There should be established an international organization under the title of The United Nations, the Charter of which should contain provisions necessary to give effect to the proposals which follow.

CHAPTER I. PURPOSES

The purposes of the Organization should be:

1. *To maintain international peace and security; and to that end to take effective collective measures for the prevention and removal of threats to the peace and the suppression of acts of aggression or other breaches of the peace, and to bring about by peaceful means adjustment or settlement of international disputes which may lead to a breach of the peace;*

2. *To develop friendly relations among nations and to take other appropriate measures to strengthen universal peace;*

3. *To achieve international cooperation in the solution of international economic, social and other humanitarian problems; and*

4. *To afford a centre for harmonizing the actions of nations in the achievement of these common ends.*

CHAPTER II. PRINCIPLES

In pursuit of the purposes mentioned in Chapter I the Organization and its members should act in accordance with the following principles:

1. The Organization is based on the principle of the sovereign equality of all peace-loving states.

2. All members of the Organization undertake, in order to ensure to all of them the rights and benefits resulting from membership in the Organization, to fulfil the obligations assumed by them in accordance with the Charter.

3. All members of the Organization shall settle their disputes by peaceful means in such a manner that international peace and security are not endangered.

4. All members of the Organization shall refrain in their international relations from the threat or use of force in any manner inconsistent with the purposes of the Organization.

5. All members of the Organization shall give every assistance to the Organization in any action undertaken by it in accordance with the provisions of the Charter.

6. All members of the Organization shall refrain from giving assistance to any state against which preventive or enforcement action is being undertaken by the Organization.

The Organization should ensure that states not members of the Organization act in accordance with these principles so far as may be necessary for the maintenance of international peace and security.

CHAPTER III. MEMBERSHIP

1. Membership of the Organization should be open to all peace-loving states.

Printed in Great Britain
by Amazon

12956707R00088